Hyde Clarke

Researches in Prehistoric and Protohistoric comparative Philology, Mythology and Archæology

in connection with the origin of culture in America and the Accad or

Sumerian families

Hyde Clarke

Researches in Prehistoric and Protohistoric comparative Philology, Mythology and Archæology
in connection with the origin of culture in America and the Accad or Sumerian families

ISBN/EAN: 9783337182502

Printed in Europe, USA, Canada, Australia, Japan

Cover: Foto ©Andreas Hilbeck / pixelio.de

More available books at **www.hansebooks.com**

RESEARCHES

IN

PREHISTORIC AND PROTOHISTORIC

COMPARATIVE PHILOLOGY,

MYTHOLOGY, AND ARCHÆOLOGY,

IN CONNECTION WITH THE

ORIGIN OF CULTURE IN AMERICA

AND THE

ACCAD OR SUMERIAN FAMILIES,

BY

HYDE CLARKE,

MEM. OF THE ANTHROPOLOGICAL INSTITUTE; COR. MEM. AMERICAN ORIENTAL SOCIETY AND OF THE BYZANTINE PHILOLOGICAL SOCIETY; FOR. MEM. OF THE AMERICAN ANTHROPOLOGICAL INSTITUTE.

LONDON:

PUBLISHED BY N. TRÜBNER & CO.,

57 & 59, LUDGATE HILL, E C.

1875.

CONTENTS.

CONTENTS—(*continued*).

PREFACE.

THE following work contains a summary of various researches in their practical application. The substance of it was read in the Session of 1874, before the Anthropological Institute; but the paper as here given, and published in the Journal, includes the results of subsequent investigations. This process has not tended to consolidate, but rather to disturb the growth.

At the same time it is the development of long preceding studies. When in Asia Minor, I soon began to see that the Hellenic theories were insufficient to explain the phenomena of Greek Asia, or even of Hellas itself, notwithstanding that so much of mythology and of geography had been made to take an Hellenic shape. Investigations in the track of my late friend, Von Halm, as to the Albanian languages, afforded no better solution. It was not difficult to recognise, what so many subsequent discoveries have compelled most men to acknowledge, that monuments and still more enduring myths, and to my sight even men, were to be found throughout Western Asia, belonging to epochs far anterior to the Hellenic migrations.

At length, as an old student of comparative philology, I sought by its methods to institute a systematic and laborious exploration of the facts and phenomena. My attention was directed to the Caucasus, as one neighbouring territory of

Lesser Asia, and particularly to the living Georgian languages, and the traces of its possible existence in ancient times. Thus I was led to examine and adopt the opinions of Brian Hodgson, Latham, Prichard, and Edwin Norris, as to the Himalayan connection of Georgian. These were barren at the time, but they afterwards helped me to a better solution. I was fortunate, too, in obtaining some glimmering light as to the river and other names.

The conduct of these researches had not been, as it may have appeared to some, desultory or wild. The necessity of investigating facts in all their bearings, very often with none but negative results, necessarily extended the field of exploration, and laid open many collateral paths. It will be seen that Georgian had already been treated as allied to Himalayan languages, and the more I applied myself to the classification of the Caucasian languages, the furthur afield did it become necessary to go. The work, too, was as much that of a linguist as of a philologist, as it was necessary to apply to the living polyglot dialects of the Caucasus a practical acquaintance with the idioms of the east and of the west, as well as many of those of antiquity. Where Greek once prevailed, Georgian, Armenian, Russian, and above all Turkish, are now found to exert an influence.

In a field so new, not only was no encouragement to be met, but, as every statement was received with the stubborn suspicion of ignorance, it became necessary to keep back facts, and, allowing for the crude state of philology, to check results as far as possible by all allied studies, anthropology, mythology, archæology, by the modicum of muddied and muddled history.

It was not self-encouraging to find that there were secret and unknown influences, languages still undetected, which might be the real and affective causes, even when a happy hit

had been made as to some individual facts. It was necessary
to publish what might be inexact, and might be erroneous, in
order to lay open the ground for investigation, and yet with
small hope of getting the help of other scholars.

At an early period, a connection became evident between
the Nile region and the Caucasus, and that with High Asia
being already acknowledged, it necessarily followed that the
Caucasus could not be the centre of migration, but only a point
of passage in the general migrations of the world.

While keeping attention on these main points, it appeared
necessary and useful to institute an exploration for the comparison of the main roots of all recorded languages, of which
about eleven hundred were available. For this purpose, a formula of comparison was devised, which materially abridged the labour; but it frequently became necessary to submit a single word
to the comparison of several hundred languages, before a safe
result could be obtained. Thus, indications for classification
were reached which were the foundations of the classification
and chronology here laid down. With this view, too, it appeared
desirable to discard the consideration of the later comparative
grammars, and to build up a knowledge ·of the prehistoric
epochs from the languages of savages, whose culture was
being turned to such good account by many able men.

In the early period, the difficulties in getting at facts were
the greater, because the word sought was sometimes concealed
under a mythological influence in one or more shapes; in time
these very circumstances afforded safer criteria; and now that
a knowledge of the various equivalents of words and roots has
been obtained, as shown in the Table of Equivalents at Page 21,
the task is much simplified. It was the more necessary to
obtain some assurance in one's own mind, because there is a
strong prejudice among men of science against philology, not
only on account of the vagaries consequent on the immature

condition of this branch of science, but because there is a strong prejudice among those addicted to material studies, and even among some philologists, that a word has no vitality or permanence. There are some who will allow such to a myth, and most willingly to a flint weapon, or a skull. There is, further, this obstacle, that a philologist is suspected of knowing nothing more than the words he picks up in a vocabulary or dictionary; and a linguist is worse off, for he is supposed to have lost solidity and accuracy the more languages he knows, and to have lost originality and individuality the better he adopts a foreign idiom.

Thus, excluded by my own profession from the world of science, it appeared to me that it might be useful in the interests of knowledge as a whole, to bring archaic philology into union with those nascent studies of anthropology, archæology, and mythology, which have met with acceptance and popularity. It cannot be pretended that this has been altogether accomplished, but a useful preparation may have been made, if in some cases a connection has been established with the text books of others. An example of this will be found in the frequent intercommunion, so far as prehistoric grammar is concerned, with the discoveries of Mr. Tylor in the field of prehistoric culture.

With so much that has been discovered as to community of origin between the new world and the old, which has become of more importance in consequence of the frequent detection of remarkable monuments, there is a hesitation in the minds of many, because it is believed, or wished to be believed, that America is an original centre of its inhabitants and their civilizations.

My treatise on the Ude language of the Caucasus and its connection with Egyptian and Coptic, published by Messrs. Trübner, and in the Journal of the Anthropological Institute, contains a statement of the connection of the Agaw of the Nile, and the Abkhass of the Caucasus, with the Omagua and Guarani of Brazil. Although the subject of the Agaw languages and migrations is reserved for another treatise, which is prepared, the subject is carried further here.

A temptation to examine the Hamath characters, and to establish their title as inscriptions, led me to explorations, very useful in these inquiries, and of which some account was given in the Journal of the Palestine Exploration Fund. This was followed in the same Journal by a paper on the river names of Palestine and the Bible, and one on town names. Other papers, communicated to the Society of Antiquaries, the Congress of Orientalists, and the British Association, show that there is a harmony among the protohistoric geographical names in Canaan, or in Italy, in Asia Minor, or in India.

Copious as are the facts already printed, and copious as are those to be found here, they are selections only from a much greater mass of facts collected, classified, and systemised during years. Thus, on the one hand, if the labour of any particular portion is hereby lessened, it must be borne in mind that my evidence on the head of topographical names or other subjects is not solely that which is here printed, but that which could conveniently be published; it is not brought together at haphazard, but in the due order and continuity of work. Those, therefore, who may be inclined to think I treat lightly the occurrence of names in Peru or New Granada, may be assured that there are few that have not been weighed by me and accepted with a due consideration of how much of chance or casual coincidence there must undoubtedly be in any such accumulation of facts.

While engaged in these pursuits, the progress of Accad studies has been a most fortunate event, for it has enabled me to employ what must be one true method in relation to the epoch under treatment. That this has been altogether justly applied, it is not for me to say, anymore than it is possible on many other matters, now for the first time, and newly, touched upon. It is true that forty years of consistent study and labour are brought to bear by me; but the subject is far too vast, and embraces too many branches of knowledge for the grasp of any one man, and particularly of one who much wants that great resource, time.

It may be asked by some,—why offer to the world statements to a certain extent new and crude, to no less a degree subject to doubt, and perhaps to disproof? It is the very necessity of the case which compels me, because the amount of truth which is inherent requires to be tested by others, and the true points in many cases can only be gathered by those who are skilled and competent. At all events, whatever may be absolutely true, there is this reason for publication, that there is much here which is true. The further evidence as to the origin of language and culture in America means also common origin with the Old World of many of the inhabitants, thereby reducing the area of the possible aborigines, and bearing on the question of the unity and development of mankind. It necessarily means the restoration, as in a palimpsest, of whole books of history long lost. If, as is respectfully submitted, the methods be right, and the facts be true, then we must remodel and constitute a prehistoric comparative philology, and we must treat with much modification the existing comparative grammars of Bopp and Caldwell, and the comparative history of Renan, and prepare the way for the comparative grammars and histories of other languages as yet supposed to be unclassified, or of which the true constituents have not been known. As an example of this, the Ugrian (at p. 11) may be taken.

In conclusion, there will be the usual objectors who want more evidence, and the men of science who allege that particular facts are not admitted by them into science. Those may be left to themselves; but if any one wishes to test the statements here made, he can do so readily, for the facts are available in accessible manuals, as those of Dr. Latham, Dr. W. W. Hunter, Col. Dalton, Colonel Lane Fox, and Sir George Campbell; and it is sincerely to be wished that many new students may be so enlisted. One point may be particularly pointed out to younger men desirous of original research and the honours and dangers of discovery, that if some out of the thousands who are learning Sanskrit grammar, and getting not one step beyond, will take up the language of a savage tribe, ample reward will be obtained. These languages of the living are the records of generations dead ages ago; and these words which have come from mouth to ear in longest time, breathe the thoughts of early worlds.

HYDE CLARKE.

32, St. George's Square, S.W.
January 6th, 1875.

RESEARCHES IN PREHISTORIC AND PROTOHISTORIC COMPARATIVE PHILOLOGY, ETC.

Researches *in* Prehistoric *and* Protohistoric Comparative Philology, Mythology, *and* Archæology, *in* Connection *with the* Origin *of* Culture *in* America, *and its* Propagation *by the* Sumerian *or* Akkad Families. By Hyde Clarke.

The old Spanish conquerors of the New World saw with wonder the buildings of Mexico and Peru, the seats, even then, of ancient empire. The fall of the Montezumas and of the Incas was accompanied by that of the civilization of which they were the leading representatives. The progress of the new ideas of religion and policy, together with the absorbing love of gold, rapidly outgrew and displaced the marvels of the ancient and strange regime, the less regarded because heathen.

The people, reduced to slavery, lost the practice of the higher arts, and while the palaces and temples went to ruin, or were buried under the thick growth of trees and creepers, no others were raised. The palaces of the viceroys and the churches of the missionaries were after foreign taste, and all tended to the forgetfulness of the ancient arts. Where there had been a conquering race in power, as that of the Incas, it was brought down to the same level of thraldom as its former subjects, the Aymaras, under the Spanish yoke, and all ambition and all stimulus to distinction were lost, as much as the power of bringing together thousands of labourers. As the languages were no longer written, except in catechisms, and the old hieroglyphics, quipus, were disused, after four centuries even the history that might have helped us has died off, leaving scanty and obscure remains.

The great buildings of Central and South America have been sufficiently described to be known to scholars, and their antique types have been the subject of much speculation during periods when the history of the human race, but ill-known now, was most imperfectly understood. According to the fancy of the writer, everything has been explained by reference to Egypt, to later India, or to China.

The gradual extension of exploration and settlement in the United States has, however, brought to light the fact that vast countries, which, for three hundred years at least, have been held by wandering savages, were occupied with monuments not less noteworthy and much more ancient than those to the south.

Step by step we have been brought to the conviction that the American continents have been held in times of yore by populations more or less forward, and in most cases more so than the present tribes, who have lost all knowledge of the monument builders, or attribute their works to races, which it can be ascertained, have no right to such a claim.

Strange as this state of things may seem, it can be understood with a little thought by what has happened in this island. When we dig down in the city some dozen or fifteen feet we come upon many remains of the Roman city, buried under layer and layer of house rubbish, garden mould, or the ashes of fires. Still deeper we reach bogs where are horns and bones belonging to a yet earlier time. (See Researches of Col. Lane Fox.) If we go abroad we see the hills topped with barrows, clad with thickets of trees, or bare and sharp, marking out their lines against the sky around us. In the west we see mounds of great stones, others in heaps built together, some balancing on peaks of rocks. We amused ourselves with calling these Druidic monuments, until we made out that we knew little about Druids, and that these great stone monuments were to be found in many lands beyond the reach of Druids or Celts.

Thus we learn how little we truly know of what has gone by in this island, of which we fill up every nook, and scan every yard of surface, nay turn over with spade or plough every foot of ground. We begin dimly to look back as it were on the torn-out leaves of a faded book, unknowing how to piece and patch together what should come first and what last, undoing now what seemed right yesterday, and by the help of some new found stray bit eking out a blank, or showing forth some awkward fault.

This is our state with all the help we can bring to bear, but, in the hunting grounds of the west, the bloodthirsty savage still hovers, and neither what is above ground, nor what is below, can be carefully searched by the few explorers, and it is less to be wondered at that we know anything than that we know so little.

The slow bringing to light of so many records of the past gave rise to a crowd of speculations as to the mode in which America was peopled, and as to the races to which the several classes of monuments are to be awarded. Into these speculations it is of little good now to enter, as they are mostly built up without any fair ground, as the ignorance or dreaming of each man has prompted. There is no language which has not been said to have been found in America, as well Gaelic as Chinese or Japanese, which it is alleged has proved a ready means of converse.

Closely knit with the whole matter, however, is that question of the population of America, which has busied many men of learning during long time. This takes two shapes, the assumption that the Americas contain an inborn, indigenous or original population, the other that they were peopled from the old world.

It is a strange fancy with which the offspring of Europeans are seized to believe that everything in America is great and original, seeing that they themselves are strangers in the land, seeing too how much they are dependent on the horse, ox, and sheep brought in by their forefathers, and on the grain first sown by them. The Spanish-speaking Peruvian has some excuse for this, because most of his blood is Indian, but the people of New England or Virginia are without a drop or more than a drop of the blood of the Indians, with whom they never wedded, and whom they have driven off to die out in the wilderness. Still there is this fancy, and every American is ready to believe that there is something especially American in the blood of the Indians and in their speech, and these opinions react in Europe. There are distinct animals in the western world, the puma, the llama, the condor, the alligator, the rattlesnake, the timber is other than in the east, and why should not men be so too, and of other birth? It has been generally affirmed that there is a common likeness between all Indians, however far apart, and that there is an American grammar, which is said to be recognizable in every tongue, however unlike its roots may be, and America, it may be noted, is the land of a thousand tongues, which bar converse between tribe and tribe, many of them scanty in number, and shut up in narrow bounds. The explanation, however, is to be sought in epochs of grammar, that is, in prehistoric, and not in geographical limits.

If the population of America is of home growth and aboriginal, then its civilization must be either aboriginal or imported from the east by a few people, wanderers, chiefs, or missionaries. We may at this point find standing ground. True it is, stray ships and canoes do drift across the Pacific, as they may have done over the Atlantic Ocean, but then the monuments in the south, and in the north more particularly, are so many and on such a scale that they are beyond such slender means, and show themselves as the work of great races.

Although some identifications have here been proposed, yet the great mass of the languages of America have been no more classified than are those of Africa and Caucasia. Everywhere we meet the same phenomena, better known to us in Caucasia, a number of dissimilar languages thrown together, but proceeding from dissimilar origins.

This is not peculiar to the Caucasus. We find it on the Nile, in West Africa, and in several regions of America. We do not, however, find in the New World such phenomena of wide-spread languages as in the Old World, the Chinese and the Indo-European. The only parallel we have is the Guarani branch of the Agaw in the Brazils, but the number is not comparable. A widespread language is the Malay. Next to this class is the extension of the Sumerian or Peru-Peguan.

It is, however, generally acknowledged that there is one language or race, that of the Eskimos, common to both worlds in the north of Asia and America. This is generally supposed to be that of the last comers, but it is quite within possibility that the race is very ancient, although it may have changed its language for that of a conqueror.

The Eskimo language may be regarded as among the most ancient known to us, and belongs to the groups of languages used by the short races, and of which one form is to be observed at the very other end of the Continent, in Tierra del Fuego. These again may be ascertained to be connected by various languages spoken by low populations in the Rocky Mountains, while others are to be noticed in the far east of Brazil on the Atlantic shore at Bahia.

These races, driven to the ends of the Continent and to headlands, as in the old world, are by language and by blood in some cases allied with that kind of Negritos or short races, of which the little men of the Minkopies in the Andamans, or of Bushmen in South Africa, afford a good type. These weak and low races, which may be called Pygmean, driven out by others stronger and perhaps more barbarous, in an early time covered both worlds. They only attest ancient occupation, and could not have supplied the monuments of any kind.

It is a singular thing that in one tribe of the Rocky Mountains, where the speech is akin to that of the short tribes, the men are as tall as their neighbours, but their women are marked as being very short.

Sir John Lubbock (British Association, Liverpool, Sept. 1870) has even hinted at the possibility of races allied to the Esquimaux having existed in England, and this is in conformity with the phenomena of human migrations as illustrated by language. The languages of the Akka Pygmies of the Nile (Pygmies of Herodotus), and of the Obongo of Du Chaillu, appear to belong to some included in the Carib-Dahomey.

The Austral Pygmean includes the Andaman Minkopie of Tickell; the Muskogolge or Creek, the Natchez in North America; the Alikulip and Tekeenika of Tierra del Fuego. Some Tasmanian roots appear to belong to this.

The SEPTENTRONAL PYGMEAN includes the Andaman Minkopie of Colebrooke; the Shoshoni, Utah, Comanch, Netela, Kij, etc., of North America; the Bayano and Darien of Central America; the Mayoruna, Kiriri, etc., of Brazil; the Dalla of Abyssinia; the Gonga languages, and probably the Wolof of West Africa; but of this further is said.

The POLAR PYGMEAN includes the Eskimo languages of America and Asia, and the Bushman of South Africa.

The Oonalashkan appears to be the link between the Eskimo and the Yeniseian. This latter class must be very early.

A remarkable exception to the languages of the short races is that of the Akka, already referred to.

The WOLOF has great affinities with the Pygmean. The people
. call themselves black. On the other side the Wolof appears to be in transition to Carib-Dahomey and to Vasco Kolarian.

A noticeable circumstance is that the Khond languages of Central India are allied to the Wolof, namely, the Gondi, Gayeti, Rutluk, Naikude, Kolami, Madi, Madia, Kuri, Keikadi, and Khond. These languages have been much affected by Dravidian.

The surroundings of this group are no less remarkable, being, except Savara (?), all African, namely, the Gadaba Agaw, and the Kolarian (Vasco-Kolarian) allied to the languages of West Africa, near the Wolof.

The SANDEH language is that of a remarkable people of the Nile region of the Nya Nya or Niam-Niam (Schweinfurth, Linguistische Ergebnisse). Notwithstanding the opinion of Livingstone, the people must be regarded as cannibals. Traces of their language exist in the Tasmanian and in the Sunda of Java, the Saru, the Guebese, and the Isle of Pines. Its chief ally was Tasmanian. The numerals appear to be in series of right and left hands. There is no appearance of the negative series. In animal names there are conformities with the Bongo or Dor.

The Nya Nya people sharpen their teeth. Dr. A. B. Meyer, of Manilla, in the course of a short visit, found skulls in the Philippines with the teeth so sharpened. This had been previously described by the old traveller Thevénot (" Zeitschrift für Ethnologie," No. 6, 1873). It is to be remarked that the boomerang, as illustrated by Colonel Lane Fox, in contradistinction to Darwin ("Desc. Man" ch. v, p. 183), conforms to the line of the Sandeh influence.

With the PAPUAN and AUSTRALIAN classes, I am in no position to deal definitely, except to classify them as languages of great antiquity. In both, Pygmean and Sandeh influences are to be suspected.

The KAMCHATDALE and the Koriak appear to me to have ancient and wide relations. The Rodiya of Ceylon shows some resemblance.

There is a strange coincidence with the Thug dialect of India. Five in Koriak is myllangan (equivalent to hand). In Thug, molu is five, and gona is hand.

The GARO of India appears to constitute an early class. It has affinities to Yangaro of Gonga in North-East Africa, and perhaps to the Dulla. In North America it is, perhaps, represented by the Paduca. [See Akka.]

The SOUR of Savara in India I cannot define. It stands out very distinctly among the Non-Aryan languages.

The Thug and Bogwan dialects or jargons show some connection.

The YUMA of North-West America is a curious family. It includes Cuchana, Cocamaricopa, Dieguno, Mohave, Khwakla-mayu, and Kulanapu. The latter and the Gallinomero, as hereafter said, are reputed to have affinities to the Chinese. The Itonama of South America, and possibly the Oregones, are allied to the Yuma.

The LENCA languages of Honduras, the Guajiquiro, the Opatero and Intibuca appear to be connected with the Kouri, Koama, Legba, Bagbalan, Keamba, etc.

The CARIB-DAHOMEY class includes two warlike and bloodthirsty divisions in Africa and America. In West Africa the Whydah, Dahomey, Adampi, Anfue, Krepec, Mahe, Popo. In America the Carib with Baniwa, Baree; Uanambeu, Juri; Purus, Coroato, Corope, Guato of Brazil; Cherente and Chavante of the Tocantins. To this group possibly belong the Coretu languages of the Orinoco.

Although there are many points of relationship between the Carib and the Dahomey, yet what is more assured is a connection with the Ankaras and Wun of Africa, which have a distinct affiliation with the Baniwa branch of the Carib.

To the Uanembeu and Coretu branches of the Carib, the Aino of Yesso, etc., has affinities. This class may have reached America by the northern route, and also by the Pacific.

Through the kindness of Professor Panceri, the Marchese

Antinori, and the Italian Geographical Society, I was favoured with some early specimens of the language of his two pygmies, Akkas, from the Nile region. They exhibit a conformity with the Ankaras and Wun, and with the Baniwa-Carib, also with Bongo, Moko, Cango, Rungo, and Wolof of Africa, Garo and Bodo of India, with Aino, and strangely enough with Javanese. Short races are found in Brazil.

The study of the group here named Carib-Dahomey is of great prehistoric interest.

The KICHAI and Hueco of Texas appear to be related to Iroquois, Pawnee, and Caddo.

The Nicaraguan MASAYA is related to the North American Mandan, Yankton, Winnebago, Dahkota, Osage, or Sioux.

The CHEROKEE and Catawba of North America are related to the Abiponian of the Missions of South America, Mbaya, Mbokobi, Vilela, Lule. There appears to be a relation to the Fellatah of Africa.

The KASIAS are remarkable as the builders of megalithic monuments. As yet I have not been able to affiliate this language. I have recognised resemblances to Naga, Mru, Bongo, and Begharmi. It would appear as if the constructors of megalithic and monolithic monuments. were the rude predecessors of the city and temple builders. The Kasias lie near the Indo-Chinese.

The KAFFIR and BERBER classes I am unable to deal with. Dr. W. H. Bleek has shown, with regard to the Bantu or Kaffir, not only that it has Australasian alliances, but that its formations are to be found in the Semitic and Aryan languages. In a paper read before the Ethnological Society, I showed that the language of the Guanches was to be added to the Berber.

The KAZI KUMUK of the Caucasus has affinities for the West African Kru, Yala, and Kasa.

The AGAW class is one of the most remarkable of the prehistoric epoch.

(a) The *Asiatic* branches are Caucasian (Abkhass, Avkass, Absné); in High Asia Kajunah(?); in India Gadaba(?); and the Rodiya of Ceylon(?).

(b) Australasia: Galela, etc.

(c) Africa, North: Agaw, Agawmidr, Waag, Falasha or Black Jews, Dizzela, Fertit, Shankali, Koldagi, Somanli; in the West Egbele, Olomo, Buduma, Pati, Bayon, Bagba, Bamon, etc.(p.157).

(d) America, North: Skwali, Sekumne, Tsamak; in Brazil, etc., Guarani, Tupi, Omagua, Mundrucu, Apiaca; in the Missions; Morima, Sararcca; on the Orinoco, San Pedro, Coretu.

There seems to have been anciently a European branch, the Akhaioi or Achivi, who afterwards became Hellenised. They very probably occupied Aquitania also. To the Egyptians, they were known as Akaiusha [see F. Lenormant, "Origines"]; and as sons of Ham are represented in Genesis by Havilah.

In the West, anciently they were settled near the Lesghians, Lycians, Cilicians (Kilikians), Lakonians, and Ligurians (Cush?). This class exercised a great influence in the propagation of culture. Its members seem anciently to have been all black.

To the Agaw class some Lake dwellers may be assigned. The Lake dwellers in Guiana now speak Guarani or Agau, and those of Lake Prasias were in undoubted proximity to Akhaioi, nor are the older lake sites remote from the ancient Akhaioi. [House and village = water, lake, etc.]

Many of the great rivers were probably named in the Agaw migrations, as Iberus, etc., Parana, etc. The Agaws were forerunners in America of the Sumerians. The Guarani animal names are distinctly Agaw.

A great class among the prehistoric languages, approaching the protohistoric, is the VASCO-KOLARIAN.

(a) In Europe it includes the Basque in its several forms.

(b) In Asia, Caucasian, the Lesghian, Kazi Kumuk, Akush Mizjezghi, Awar, etc.

(c) In India, the Kolarian group, Ho, Singbhum, Sontali, Bhumij, Mundari, Uraon, Kuri, Juang, etc.

(d) In Eastern Asia, Korean (?).

(e) In North Africa, the Furian.

(f) In West Africa, the Houssa, Mandingo, Bambarra, Yoruba languages, the Ebo, Ashantee and Fantee, Kossa, Fulah.

(Connected with the Akush may be the Kru, Grebo, Gbe, Dewoi, Bassa, Aro, Mbofia, Isoama, Isiele, Yala. (Compare Kazi-Kumuk).

(g) For America, I have not yet determined the members, but the Puelche of the Pampas appears to be one, and perhaps the Attakapa.

The Vasco-Kolarian has Tree and House conforming to Village and Grove. The roots for Tooth and Bone supply names for implements. The names of beasts are based on those for the dog, and altogether the early elements appear to belong to a stage when men were passing from an age of stone to one of bone, and from caves to tree dwellings.

The grammar exhibits what I have termed the Negative Series well developed. Its mythology is dual, not trinary or trinitarian, and traces of animism are defined. The early rudiments of culture are attested by the verbs.

At present, all the northern members are white or brown, and all the southern members black, but, in the time of Herodotus blacks existed as far north as the Caucasia.

One striking feature is that, notwithstanding the present social differences, the people are and have been warlike. The Basques resisted the Romans as they do the Spaniards; the Avars attacked the Roman Empire; the Lesghians, under Shamyl, resisted the Russians; the Sonthals rose in rebellion against us; the Koreans beat off the Americans and French, as they resisted the Chinese and Japanese; the Ashantees have encountered us in a war, where Houssas and Kossas also fought. The characteristic is general and persistent. The Reverend A. H. Sayce points out Basque affinities in Accad or Sumerian. These, as well as the Ugrian affinities (see Sayce and Lenormant), are most likely to be accounted for from the Hamitic relations. (See Ugrian, p. 157.)

In its Caucasian branch the Akush may stand in relation to the scheme in Genesis as Cush or Kush, with Mitzraim (Egyptian), Havilah (Agaw), and Canaan (Paleo-Georgian), that is with Accad and with Hamath. If so, these may all be treated for prehistoric purposes as Hamitic. [Comp. E. von Bunsen.]

The Vasco-Kolarian class has this attribute, that it particularly influenced the Dravidian, with which it has been assimilated by Caldwell and other authorities. Its main negative roots Gaba conform with Sumerian Paka, showing the same mental basis of formation.

The Lycian language differs from the others in Asia Minor, and, as pointed out, populations with allied names are found in proximity to those of Agaw names. M. Lenormant has suggested that Lycian and Lakonian were perhaps allied. It is possible to go further, and suggest a distinct Lesghian origin [the Georgian is Lekki], which may be referable to Peleg and Pelasgic, and may include Cilicians (Kilikians), Leleges, Lucanians, Ligurians, and Ligyes.

The Abkass and Lesghian populations may have been united in raids in the Mediterranean.

What is the exact place of the UGRIAN class, or what are its real constituents, I am unable to determine. By some it is held to include four chief branches, and is treated as Altaic, that is Finnic (including Magyar), Mongolic, Manchoo, and Turkic.

I am by no means satisfied that the connection goes further than a common subjection to the influence of a contemporaneous prehistoric epoch, affording a community of grammar and a participation in some terms of culture. For that matter, like influences, though to a slighter degree, may be recognised even in English.

So far as the Finnic or Ugrian is concerned, an important member is to be added, and that consists of tribes in East Nepaul and the frontiers of Tibet and China, including Rodong,

Rungchenbung, Chhingtangya, Nachhering, Waling, Yakha, Chourasaya, Kulungya, Thulungya, Bahinga, Lohorong, Lambichhong, Balali, Sangpang, Dumi, Khaling, Dungmali, and Kiranti in East Nepaul; Takpa and Manyak on the Chinese frontier; Sunwar, Gurung; Moormi, *Magar*, and Newar in Nepaul; and Vayu among the broken tribes of Nepaul. The languages of North-west Bengal, which are influenced by the Himalayan Ugrian, are Bodo, Borro, Kachari, and Dhimal; and the Miri (Abor and Sibsagur) of the eastern frontier of Bengal.

It will be seen that among the above names is Magar, and this and its neighbours closely approximate to Magyar, as other languages do to Fin. There is strong ground for believing that the settlement of Hungary was effected by a large body of tribes of Himalayan Ugrians, under Avar or Khunzag (Hun or Leschian) leaders. There is, however, a Hung subtribe of the Limbu. Thus a Finnic language was introduced rather from the Himalayas than from North-western Asia.

[It may be noted that on the Gaboon in Africa some affinities of language are to be traced in Bayon, Pati, Kum, Bagba, Balu, Bamon, Ngoala, Momenyah, Papiah, Param, but these also show affinity with Agaw, p. 154.]

The Rev. A. H. Sayce ("Akkad Seal" in Journal of Philology) has shown some strong resemblances between Akkad and Ugrian, particularly in pronouns and numerals, and these have been supported by M. E. Sayous and M. F. Lenormant ("Lenormant Etudes Accadiennes," vol. i, part 1, p. 200, and part 3, p. 133, also Magie, 1874). The test of pronouns accepted by philologists is very weak (see Pronouns after). In my view the affinities are not to be regarded as confined to Ugrian, because some of the alleged affinities are common to the prehistoric epoch, and others are to be attributed to the, as yet, undetermined influence, which equally affects the Tibetan and the Chinese. The relation of Georgian with Akkad is very great, and yet it is none the less so with Tibetan, as was illustrated by Bryan Hodgson, Dr. Latham, Dr. Prichard, and Edwin Norris. This view I supported, but I am inclined materially to modify it.

With regard to the Manchoo I have stated (in the Phœnix) that the few remaining Scythian words preserved by Herodotus appear to conform.

The MALAY class is to be regarded as prehistoric from the evidence of the culture of the populations, though the populations and their languages must have been largely modified by protohistoric influences, but at the same time they bear also the impress of the ruder prehistoric classes, even of the Sandeh, the Akka, and probably of the Pygmean.

The Circassian and Otomi, etc., may be either intermediate between Agaw and Sumerian, or are to be included with the latter. If so, they were outlying and advanced members, and in the occupation of America must have closely followed the Agaw.

As PROTOHISTORIC languages I propose Egyptian, Sumero-Peruvian, Chinese, Tibetan, Dravidian.

The protohistoric languages will be found to be less widely distributed than the prehistoric. With the exception of the great branches of the Sumerian (Peruvian, Mexican, etc.), and a doubtful affinity of Dravidian, they did not reach America.

It was only through the Egyptian they affected North-east Africa and West Africa, nor did they spread over Australasia.

Where the EGYPTIAN class should be placed I am unable to determine. It includes, as I have shown (" Comparative Grammar of Egyptian, Coptic, and Ude," in "Journal of Anthropological Institute," 1873), the Ude language of the Caucasus. Its characteristics are those of remote antiquity. Leo Reinisch, in his laborious work on the unity of language (Vienna, 1874), has illustrated the connections of the Egyptian and Coptic with the Teda or Tibbu class. With this subject Dr. Carl Abel of Berlin is now dealing.

Thus we obtain a conformity of ethnographical facts, observed elsewhere, for we should find Mitzraim in the neighbourhood of Kush in a North African centre.

The SUMERO-PERUVIAN class will be dealt with in detail in the after part of this memoir.

The CHINESE class requires to be more carefully studied, because, as the Chinese has been influenced by other earlier civilizations, there has been a fancy to give to similar phenomena in other languages, or in other culture, a Chinese origin. The alleged influence of Chinese in America is referred to hereafter as more probably Sumerian.

Of the TIBETAN class the same remark is to be made. Thus the followers of Bryan Hodgson, including myself, have included under Tibetan what will most likely have to be separated, certainly the Himalayo-Ugrian. A common religious influence, as in the case of Islam, is very apt to lead to similar and common appearances in language and culture.

As regards the DRAVIDIAN class my object is to avoid entering into detail. I believe its influence to be much smaller in truth than what Caldwell and other Indian authorities, looking at it from a Tamil stand point, have been inclined to attribute to Dravidian. Vasco-Kalarian has greatly influenced this class.

To Dravidian should most likely be referred Japanese and Loochoo, which have likewise Basque similarities. The Brahui (Caldwell, p. 25) has Tamil affinities (Felice Finzi, Il Brahui, 1870).

The Circassian of the Caucasus and the Chetemacha of North America show some affinity to Dravidian, but the Circassian is allied to the Othomi of Mexico, and is for the present classed with Sumerian.

As yet, I have failed to account for an important period in language and culture, which greatly influenced the historic period. Passing beyond the dual system, or more properly that of pairs and positive and negative elements, a sacred system of three was introduced. In grammar we have these triple forms. and triliteral roots, the latter in Semitic and the other in Aryan. Mythology was greatly affected by a trinitarian and triune system, embracing one great member, one male and one female.

In grammar, there are three parts (noun, verb, and participle), three nouns (noun, adjective, and pronoun), three numbers, three cases, three degrees, three verbs (active, neuter, or middle, and passive), three persons, three tenses, three moods, three participles, three particles (adverb, preposition and conjunction), three concords.

As HISTORIC languages, I classify Semitic, Aryan.

As my present programme is to deal with the earlier stages of language, this epoch is passed by. It is, however, necessary to observe that many roots and characteristics, which are regarded as Semitic or Aryan, are in reality prehistoric, and that for the consideration of the prehistoric and protohistoric periods, the historic aspect is generally useless or mischievous. The same remark applies equally to mythology and philology. It is also untrue that Sanskrit in itself affords evidence as to the early culture of mankind, apart from the prehistoric languages.

These classes of languages, prehistoric and protohistoric, are now chiefly found in various regions, which in some periods have been centres of migration, and in others centres of refuge for the earlier races driven in by those more powerful of the protohistoric and historic epochs.

The chief of these regions are:—High Asia, Caucasia, North East Africa (Nile), West Africa, India, North-East Asia, North America, Central America, South America.

The distribution and order of succession may thus be represented:— (See next page.)

The relations of High Asia may thus be briefly represented:

	High Asia.	Caucasus.	Africa.	America.
Agaw or Havilah ...	... Kajunah	... Avkhas	... Agaw	... Omagua
Ugrian	... E.Nepaul,Turk, Mongol ...	—	Bayon, etc. ...	—
Egyptian	... (Mitzraim)	... Ude ...	... Egyptian ...	—
Sumerian	... (Unknown)	... Georgian? ...	—	Peruvian, etc.
Chinese	... Chinese ...	—	—	—
Tibetan	... Tibetan ...	—	—	—
Ayran ...	... Dard ...	... Ossetinian ...	—	—

	North America.	Central America.	South America.	North Africa.	West Africa.	Australasia.	Asia.	India.	Caucasia.	Europe.
PREHISTORIC.										
Pygmean, Austral	Creek									
„ Septentrion	Shoshon	Darien	T. del Fuego							
„ Polar	Eskimo		Mayoruna	Gouga	Bushman	Andaman	Eskimo			(Lap?)
Wolof (Carib?)					Wolof	Andamsu (Tasman.)		Khond		
Sandeh	Paduca			Sandeh						
Garo (Carib?)				Yangaro	Kouri	(Tasman?)		Garo		
Lenca		Lenca	Coretu	Akka	Dahomey	(Java?)	Aino	(Garo?)		
Carib			Carib	Agaw	Egbele?	Galela	Kajunah	Gadaba Rodiya		
Agaw	Skwali		Omagua	Furian				Kolarian	Avkhass	Akhaioi?
Vasco-Kolarian	Attakapa?		Puelche		Houssa		Korean	E. Nepaul	Lesghian	Basque
Ugrian					Bamon,		Ostiak		Nogai?	Magyar
Malay				Madagas-[car	—[etc.	Malay				—
PROTOHISTORIC.										
Egyptian	} Mexican			Egyptian	Tibboo		Akkad	Peguan	Ude	
Sumerian	} Othomi, etc.	Maya	Aymara, etc.				IndoChina		Georgian?	Etrus-[can?]
Chinese							Chinese		Circassian	
Tibetan							Tibetan	Tibetan		
Dravidian	Chetemacha?						Japanese	Tamil		
HISTORIC.										
Semitic				Subsemit			Semitic			
Aryan							E. Aryan	Aryan	Ossetinian	W. Aryan

There can be no reasonable doubt that High Asia is a centre to which in ancient times, on the west Caucasia, the Nile and West Africa conformed, as India did to the south; but it has been denuded of its early black races, and of many later. For instance, the number of Aryans is very small.

From High Asia, Caucasia was supplied to the west, and thence the African regions, which present a parallel. To the south are found India and Australasia, and to the east, North east Asia, North America, Central America, and South America. If the southern margins, including Aaros, etc., were taken, we should obtain early prehistoric members.

The following shows the relations of the Caucasian centre:

	Caucasia.	W. Africa.	N. Africa.	Europe.
	Kazi Kumuk	Kru ...	—	—
Agaw or Havilah ...	Avkhass ...	—	Agaw	... (Akhaioi)
Vasco-Kolarian or Cush	Lesghian ...	Houssa..	Furian	... (Ligurian?)
	—	—	—	Basque
Egyptian or Mitzraim .	Ude... ...	Tibbu ...	Mitzraim ...	—
Sumerian or Canaan ...	Georgian ...	—	—	Etruscan?
"	Circassian ...	—	—	—
Dravidian	—	—	—	—
Aryan	Ossetinian...	—	—	W. Aryans

	High Asia.	India.	America.
Agaw or Havilah ...	Kajunah ...	Gadaba? ...	Omagua
Vasco-Kolarian or Cush	—	Kolarian ...	Puelche?
Egyptian or Mitzraim..	(Mitzraim?) ...	—	—
Sumerian or Canaan ...	(Akkad) ...	Peguan ...	Peruvian
"	—	—	Othomi
Dravidian	—	Dravidian ...	—
Aryan	Dard	Aryans ...	—

The languages and mythology of High Asia were reproduced, and their parallels were found in Caucasia, which came in the historical school of Babylon to be regarded as the Paradise or cradle of the human race. The migrations were transferred to the Nile region, and at a later day the localities were mixed up with those of Caucasia and High Asia.

The following shows the relations of the Nile centre:

	N. Africa.	W. Africa.	Europe.	Caucasia.
Pygmean	... Gonga ...	—	—	—
Sandeh ...	... Sandeh ...	—	—	—
Garo ...	... Yangaro ...	—	—	—.
Khasia ...	... Bongo ...	Begharmi ...	—	—
Agaw ...	... Agaw ...	Egbele ...	(Akhaioi) ...	Avkhass
Egyptian	... Egyptian ...	Tibbu ...	—	Ude
Semitic ...	... Subsemitic...	—	—.	—

C

	High Asia.	India.	Australia.	America.
Pygmean ...	—	—	Andaman ...	Shoshon
Sandeh	—	—	Tasmania ...	—
Garo	—	Garo ...	(Java?) ...	Paduca?
Khasia	—	Khasia ...	—	—
Agaw	Kajunah ...	Gadaba ...	Galela ...	Omagua
Egyptian ...	—	—.	—	—
Semitic	—	—	—	—

The Nile region must be looked upon as the transmitting station for West Africa.

The following shows the relations of West Africa, as a centre of language and population:

	W. Africa.	N. Africa.	Caucasia.	India.
Wolof	Wolof ...	—	—	Khond
Lenca-Kouri ...	Kouri ...	—	—	—
Carib-Dahomey .	Dahomey ...	Akka ...	—	Garo
„	(Fellatah?)...	—	—	—
„	Kru... ...	—	Kazi-Kumuk	—
Agaw	Egbele, etc...	Agaw ...	Avkhass ...	Gadaba
Vasco-Kolarian ..	Houssa, etc..	Furian ...	Lesghian ...	Kol
Ugrian ...	Bayon, etc...	—	—	E. Nepaul
Egyptian	Tibboo? ...	Egyptian ...	Ude... ...	—

	Asia.	N. America.	C. America.	S. America.
Wolof	—	—	—	—
Lenca-Kouri ...	—	—	Lenca ...	Coretu?
Carib-Dahomey ..	Aino ...	—	—	Carib
„	—	Catawba ...	—	—
„	—	—	—	—
Agaw	Kajunah ...	Skwali ...	—	Om-agua
Vasco-Kolarian ..	—	Attakapa?...	—	Puelche?
Ugrian ...	Ugrian ...	—	—	—
Egyptian ...		—	—	—

It will be seen that the copious series of West African classes are transmitted from the east, and must have traversed the Nile region; and the barbarism of W. Africa is attributable to its non-participation in the higher migrations.

Passing from High Asia to the south, we have to consider the relations of India as a centre, which are thus illustrated:

	India.	Africa.	Caucasia.	America.	Misc.
Wolof ...	Khond	Wolof ...	—	Carib ...	—
Kamchatdale ...	Thug ...	—	[ka —	—	Kamchat-
Garo ...	Garo	Yangaro,Ak-	—	Paduca, N...	— [dale
Khasia ...	Khasia	Bongo ...	—	—	—
Agaw ...	Gadaba	Agaw	Avkhas	Omagua, S...	—
„ ...	Rodiya	Egbele	—	Skwali, N....	—
Vasco-Kolarian.	Kol	Houssa	Lesghian	Puelche?	Korean
Ugrian	E. Nepaul.	Bayon	—	—	Ugrian
Sumerian	Cambojan .	—	Georgian?	Peruvian	Indo-China
„	Peguan ...	—	Circassian?.	Othomi	... —
Tibetan	Tibetan ...	—	—	—	Tibetan
Dravidian	Tamil ...	—	—	—	Japanese?
Aryan ...	Aryan ...	—	Ossetinian...	—	W. Aryan

In the prehistoric period there was an absolute conformity between India and Africa, which is confirmed by collateral ethnological facts.

From India was most probably the route of departure for Australasia, and for Indo-China, and through these to America in the later epochs.

North-east Asia constituted a centre of passage for migration.

	N. E. Asia.	America.	Africa.
Pygmean	Eskimo	... Eskimo	... Bushman
Carib	Aino ...	... Carib ...	... Dahomey
Agaw	?	Om-agua	... Agaw
Vasco-Kolarian	Korean	... Puelche?	... Houssa, etc.
Dravidian	Japanese	... Chetemacha?...	—

The Agaw class appears to have left no representatives in north-east Asia, nor did the Sumerian. They are, however, most developed in the southern regions of America. It is to be inferred that whilst the other and earlier migrations passed over Behring's Straits, the latter passed over the Pacific by Easter Island. The mound builders may have passed over by the northern route, but they may have been intermediate between the Sumerian and Agaw migrations.

The relation of the languages of America with those of the old world has been exhibited at each stage, but the comparison is shown in a succeeding table, and which represents an affinity of at least a hundred languages on each side.

Languages common to America and the Old World.

		America.		Old World.
Pygmean	...	Creek, Natchez, N.	...	Mincopie
,,	...	T. del Fuego ...	...	
,,	...	Shoshoni, N., Darien, C....		Mincopie
,,	...	Mayoruna, S. ...	...	Gonga, Afr.
,,	...	Eskimo, N. ...	...	Eskimo
Garo	...	Paduca? N. ...	...	Garo, Yangaro, Afr.
Lenca-Kouri	...	Honduras, C. ...	...	Kouri, Afr.
Carib-Dahomey	...	Carib, S. ...	...	Dahomey, Afr. Aino
Agaw	...	Omagua, S. ...	...	Agaw, Afr. Avkhas
Vasco-Kolarian	...	Puelche? S. ...	...	Houssa, Afr. Kol
,,	...	Attakapa? N. ...	...	
Sumerian	...	Maya, Mexican, C.	...	Indo-Chinese
,,	...	Peruvian, S. ...	...	Akkad
,,	...	Othomi, N. ...	...	Circassian

With the absolute chronology of these successions I do not propose to deal. Three thousand years ago, the Sumerian race had come in contact with the Semitic, to which it had to succumb. Seven hundred years later is perhaps to be taken as the epoch of conflict with the Aryan race. This, however, gives us no real instrument of measure. We do not sufficiently know how far the members of the Hamitic classes are to be regarded as synchronous.

c 2

This is to be observed, on the other hand, that it must have taken long periods for races so weak as the Pygmean to have permeated the world, penetrating to Tierra del Fuego by traversing Behring's Straits and the whole Pacific coast of the Americas.

Although the Sumerians were assailed by the Semites three thousand years ago they were only overcome by the Spaniards four hundred years since and in Indo-China they still flourish. The question, therefore, is not the duration of culture in the form of language, but what are the spaces required for its development.

If the Sumerian settlement in Babylonia took place four thousand years ago (see Ernest de Bunsen, " Chronology of the Bible") then the settlement in India would be of the same date, if the migration was from a common centre in High Asia, as the division of West and East Sumerian in pronouns and other details seems to indicate.

The settlements in Indo-China would shortly follow, and afterwards the occupation of Java and the islands.

It is quite within compass that Pera was reached three thousand years ago, or even four or five thousand. It is to be observed that the Malay occupation of Australasia must have cut off the Sumerian intercourse with America. Then it is to be taken into consideration that if the intercourse had been kept up at a time when large ships were used by the Phœnicians, Chinese, Greeks, Romans or Arabs, we should have witnessed different conditions. Cattle and horses would have been carried across the Pacific. Had the intercourse from Indo-China to South America been fresh in the memory the Arab navigators would have heard of it.*

There is a prevalent notion among naturalists that words are perishable and cannot be transmitted, but that is founded on an erroneous conception, particularly of facts stated by Mr. A. R. Wallace. It is certainly true that under some circumstances words are subject to mutation, but even in this respect there are mostly limits to mutation; but it is, nevertheless, certain that words can be transmitted for thousands of years. So far as the Sumerian is concerned words written three or four or five thousand years ago in Babylonia, where the language is extinct, are preserved in an unwritten form by American populations. Still longer periods must have passed for the diffusion of the identical words in the Kolarian of India and of Houssa, and more still for the period of diffusion of Wolof in Africa and Khond in India.

---

* It is possible that the legend of the roc, in Sindbad's voyages, may refer to the condor, and that there may be other traditions traceable besides those of the four worlds, and the later Chinese intercourse treated of by the Abbé Pipart (Congress of Orientalists, 1873, p. 187) and by Mr. C. G. Leland.

To naturalists, I would particularly point out the names of animals common to South America and Central Africa.

The observance of these facts and of the law resulting therefrom is of great importance in the whole history of culture, because they give us a life for a word or for a myth, as for a race, and in many cases the word or the myth is more purely preserved from intermixture than the cranial forms.

It will thus be seen that the way in which I propose to deal with the prehistoric and proto-historic periods is other than the methods adopted in the valuable works of Sir John Lubbock, Mr. Tylor, Professor Reinisch, or Professor Frederick Muller, and that collaterally and by a parallel path, I follow the investigations of Colonel Lane Fox and Mr. J. Evans. If I go beyond these, I do not enter on the domain of later philology and mythology, which has been occupied with so much learning and ingenuity by Professor Max Müller and others.

PREHISTORIC COMPARATIVE PHILOLOGY is closely connected with comparative mythology, and the two subjects illustrate each other. It would, therefore, be well if the term cultural philology could be employed.

In the prehistoric period an idea was represented by three or four words, and, again, a word was represented by three or four ideas. Thus we find that words or roots are interchangeable, and it is necessary to study their morphology, for the purpose of understanding the equivalents and real connection of roots in various languages.

Table of Equivalents of Roots and Words.

Above	... Sky, day	Black	... (Negative series)
Acorn	... Stone, bead ?		Not, night
Air ...	... Breath, wind, soul, sky		1 ? 6 ?
Ant ..	... Bug, fire ?		Tribal name (Wolof)
Arm ...	... Hand, foot, leg	Blood	... Head, red, water
Arrow	... Bone, tooth, horn, bird	Boat, ship	... Fish, box, bowl, plough
	Lance, knife, axe, hatchet (death?)	Bone...	... Rib, leg, tooth, horn
			Tree, arrow, spear, white ?
Anger	... Arrow		
Axe (see hatchet)		Born...	... (negative) Child
Bad ...	... Not (negative series), Not good [night	Bow ...	... Arrow
		Bowl...	... Boat
Bat ...	... Bird	Box ...	... Boat
Bead...	... Egg, bean, pea	Boy ...	... Child, son, born
Bean...	... Bead, pea, egg	Breath	... Air, wind, soul
Bear...	... Teeth	Brother	... Father, uncle
Beard	... Mouth, hair, nose		Sister
Bee ...	... Honey fly		Side
Before	... Mouth	Bull ...	... Elephant, stag, cow, tooth, tusk, horn
Belly	... Womb		
Bird ...	} (Negative series)	Calf ...	... Oxchild
Fowl	} Foot, leg, hand, rat	Cat (phonetic)	
Bitter	... Sour, bad	Chief, see king	

Child	... Mouth? son, born		Fowl (see bird)	
Claw...	... Foot, nail		Fox ...	... Dog, kite
Cow ...	... (Negative series)		Girl ...	... Daughter, woman
	Woman		Go ...	... Eat, drink, run, move
	Mother bull, ox woman		Goat...	... Ewe (negative series)
	Ewe, goat			Dog
Crow (phonetic) Blackbird, dog			God ...	... Name, sky, fire
Cuckoo (phonetic)			Gold...	... Sun, snake
Dart...	... Snake, lance		Grain	... Field
Daughter	... Son, born		Green	... Black, yellow, grass
	Girl, woman, mother		Hair ...	... Tooth? Star?
	Cow			Head
Day ...	... Sun, light, sky, above, 5			Thread, cord, stuff, wool
Dead	... (Negative series)		Hand	... Foot, arm, leg, fowl, 5
Dog ...	... Horse, cat, hog, eagle,		Hatchet	... Knife, arrow
	cow, fish, snake		Hawk	... Fox
Door...	... Mouth, word, speak,		He, they	... Man, 3
	house		Head	... Hair
Dove	... Eagle [tive]			Man, chief, king
Dream	... Death, sorcerer (nega-			Mountain, stone, foot,
Drink	... Eat, speak, go, within			finger
Dumb	... (Negative)		Hear...	... Ear
Dust...	... Earth, sand		Heart	... Blood, hearth, house,
Eagle	... Wolf, dog, rat, dove			earth, hair, liver, lung
Ear ...	... (Negative series)		Heaven	... See sky
	Egg, sun?		Here...	... This, thou
	Hear		Hog ...	... Dog, goat, horse, fat?
Earth	... Heart		Hoof...	... Foot
Eat ...	... Drink, speak, go, within		Hoopooe (phonetic)	
Eel ...	... Snake, fish		Horn...	... Nose, bone, tooth, ar-
Egg ...	... Bird, fowl			row, ship, elephant,
	Bead, bean, pea, round			etc.
	Ear		Horse	... Dog, hog, snake, sun,
Eight	... 4, 2, 5 + 3 (otherhand 3)			run
Elephant	... Tooth, bone, bull, stag		House	... Heart?
End ...	... Tail			Tree
Executioner . (Negative series)				Mouth, door
Ewe ...	... (Negative series)		I, me...	... One
	Cow, woman		Iron ...	... Hard
Eye ...	... Mouth, face		King...	... Head
	Man, I		Kite ...	... Fox, dog
	Sun		Knife	... Arrow, lance, hatchet
	See, water		Lake...	... River, house
Face...	... Mouth, eye, nose		Lance	... Tongue, dog
Far ...	... Long			Arrow, knife, hatchet
Fat ...	... Oil, hog?		Leaf ...	... Flower, tongue
Father	... Mother, brother, man		Leg ...	... Foot, hand, bone
Feather	... Tongue (leaf?)		Light	... Day, fire, sun
Female	... (Negative series)		Lion ...	... Dog
Field	... Grain		Liver	... Lung
Finger	... Teat, head of hand		Long...	... Far
Fire ...	... Sun, light, day, God?		Lord, see king	
	animal names		Man ...	... Father, head, Woman
Fish ...	... Snake, dog, bird? sun,			Eye, sun
	Ship, boat			He, they
Five ...	... Iland, sun			(Tribe name)
Flower	... Leaf		Mare...	... (Negative series)
Fly ...	... Mouse? bug, ant		Milk ...	... Water, water x
Foot ...	... Hand, arm, leg, head		Mill ...	... Stone
Forest	... Village		Mole...	... Nose
Four...	... 2, 8, 9, many		Monkey	... Above

Moon	... Mother, mouth, woman,
	(negative series)
	Sun, star
	Skywoman, night eye
	Red, two
Mother	... Father
	Woman, wife
	Moon, mouth
Mountain	... Head
Mouse	... Fly? rat
Mouth	... Word, speech, tongue
	Mother, moon, woman
	Before
	Door
	Child
Move...	... Go, run
Nail ...	... Thorn
Naked	... (Negative series)
Name	... Sun, God (negative?)
Nerve	... String, vein
Nest ...	... Egg, womb (negative?)
Night (negative series).	Not, night
	Black
	Kill, executioner
	Female
Nine ...	... 5 + 4, 4 of other hand
No, not	... (Negative series)
	Not, yes
Nose ...	... Horn, beard, mole, head
Nut ...	... Egg (negative series)
Oil ...	... Fat
One ...	... I, me
	White? black?
Ostrich	... Snakebird, birdsnake
Pea ...	... (See bean)
Phallus	... (See tail)
Plough	... Ship
Pound	... Stone, mill
Rat ...	... Mouse, wolf, eagle, bird,
	snake
Red ...	... Blood
	Two (negative series),
	seven?
Rib ...	... Bone, side (=woman?)
River	... Water, water running,
Round	... Egg [village
Run ...	... Go
Salt ...	... Sour
Sand...	... Dust, earth
See ...	... Eye
Seven	... 5 + 2, two of other hand,
	red? white?
Shadow	... Soul, eclipse (negative)
Sheep	... Goat, see ewe
Shell...	... Skull
Ship ...	... Fish, plough, horn
Sister	... Brother, daughter
	Woman-brother, wo-
	man-cow?
Six ...	... 5 + 1, one of other hand

Skull...	... Shell, headshell
Sky ...	... Above, day, sun, air,
	mountain
Snake	... Fish, rat, horse, dog
,,	... Dart
,,	... Sun, gold
Snow	... (Negative series)
Son ...	... Child, boy, water
Sorcerer	... Dream, death
Soul ...	... Breath, wind, air, sha-
	dow
Spark	... Star
Speak	... Mouth, door, before,
	eat, drink
Spear	... See lance
Spittle	... Mouthwater
Stag ...	... Bull, elephant, goat,
	horn, etc.
Star ...	... Sun, moon, spark, ani-
	mal names·
Stone	... Rock, tooth, stool
	Pound, mill
	Acorn
	Head
Stool...	... Stone
String	... Thread, hair, nerve
Sun ...	... Day, fire, light, sky
	Moon, star
	Skyeye, Skyman
	Eye, nose, man
	Animal, dog, snake,
	fish
	Gold
	5
	Yes
	Name
Swan	... Dog
Sword	... Knife, stick
Tail ...	... Phallus, end
Teat ...	... Finger
Tear ...	... Eyewater
Ten ...	... Foot, hand
Tendon	... See Nerve
This ...	... Thou
Thorn	... Nail
Thou...	... This, that, 2
Three	... Black? He?
Tiger	... Dog, sun, fire
Tongue	... Mouth, speech, knife,
	lance, leaf
Tooth	... Bone, horn, arrow
	Elephant, bear
Tree ...	... Wood, tooth? bone?
	House, village
Two ...	... Red (negative series)
Vein ...	... Nerve
Village	... Forest, tree, river, lake
Water (nega-	[village
tive series).	River, child, eye, house,
White	... One, seven, bone
Wife ...	... Motherman *see* (woman)

Wind	... Breath, air, soul			Mouth, yona, moon
Window	... Hole	Womb	... Belly	
Wing	... Ear	Wood	... See tree	
Within	... Eat, drink	Wool...	... Hair	
Wolf...	... Dog	Word	... Mouth, speak, door	
Woman(nega-		Yes ...	... Light, day, sun, not-no	
tive series) .	Man	Yona...	... Woman, mouth, moon	
	Wife, mothergirl			

Among the earliest forms of words and those most widely distributed and longest preserved are those for parent, at a later date discriminated into father and mother. The complex relations of kindred and of terms for it have been well treated by Sir John Lubbock.

The Georgian language presents one example of the inversion of the usual distribution in Sumerian and other classes, mama being father, and deda, mother.

In no department, perhaps, is the bearing of equivalent roots more strongly seen than in ANIMAL names.

In Vasco-Kolarian many names of animals are allied to Kari, dog, and this phenomenon is to be seen throughout.

This root appears to be allied to Kurritcea Basque, to run. In some languages the stork is named from being a runner. In prehistoric philology fowl is allied to foot and leg, most likely from running.

One true origin of animal names is perhaps to be found in a passage of Herodotus, iii, 16, dwelt upon by Mr. Tylor, "Early History of Mankind," p. 235. It runs, "By the Egyptians also it hath been held that fire is a living beast, and that it devours everything it can seize, and when filled with food it perishes with what it has devoured."

Being led to test this I found the word fire to conform with dog and tiger in Hunter's "New Aryan Dictionary," and further, sun and star to conform. This I ascertained to be a general law of prehistoric language. If the word tiger be taken, the forms, although conforming also to dog, are mostly sun forms.

Snake conforms to sun in virtue of the same law, and hence its place in nature-worship with the sun.

As the sun and stars have movement it is to be conceived that men were led to assimilate to them the moving animals, beasts, birds, and snakes. As fire is allied to the sun, and as fire eats, so too was a conformity found with devouring beasts of prey.

It is by no means impossible that the idea being so taken the phonetic was obtained from crow, which gives the forms ka, kawa, kali, koura, klah.

It may be a question whether the cock or the crow gave name to birds, for though Mr. Tylor ("Primitive Culture," i, 207) quotes akoka in Ebo, kuku in Zulu, and kukko in Finnish for the cock, yet kaka is a wide name for the crow, and the same form has supplied the word for cuckoo too.

It is within compass that positive and negative names in the form of sun and moon-names may have furnished many epithets, the sun for names of male animals, the moon or mother for female animals. It is certainly the case for female animals, but on account of common names being used for male and female, it is difficult to discriminate in all instances.

The word for tiger in " Hunter's Dictionary" is so commonly a sun word, that we may in this way, from verbal mythology, obtain some notion why the tiger is so mysteriously regarded in India. This does not, however, support weather or cloud mythology.

It is possible that the Egyptian doctrine may be applicable to the Akkad cases, where L is an animal characteristic (as in man, mulu; mother, luku; stag, lulum; sheep, lu; some beast, lubat; bull, la; dog and lion, liku). Sun is, however, lakh; moon, lid; light, lik; and eye, lim. There are traces of the same phenomena in Aymara and in Mexican. This syllable appears to exist in Indo-European and Semitic as in lupus, lepus, alopex, leo, lagos, lukus; aleph, elephas, elaphros.

With the sun idea I should be inclined to connect the fact that with the Algonquins (Tylor, "Primitive Culture", i, 302) not only all animals belong to the animate gender, but also the sun, moon, and stars. The animate gender includes trees and fruits, and, besides, the altar, sacrifice stone, the bow, the eagle and feather, the kettle, tobacco pipe, drum, and wampum.

In Genesis ii, 19, etc., it is said of every beast of the field and fowl of the air that " whatsoever Adam called every living creature that was the name thereof. And Adam gave names to all cattle and to the fowl of the air, and to every beast of the field."

This appears to preserve the tradition, that in the prehistoric epoch man did name the beasts and birds, the system pursued being still recognisable.

The names of beasts being founded on the type of the dog, names of birds are founded on those of beasts.

It can readily be understood how the vulture is named after the tiger, the hawk after the fox. The ostrich is a snake bird, the swan a dog, and swine.

Insects are also named after beasts.

In the same way the snake is assimilated to the horse, rat, and fish, as it is to the sun.

The fish is the equivalent of the horse and snake, the eel is a snake-fish.

The bat is a bird.

Of distinctive names for animals are to be noted, for elephant, tooth; for bear, teeth; for mole, nose; for horse, runner; for fowl, leg and foot.

Other equivalents will be found in the foregoing table of equivalents.

The names of animals are in some cases obtained from combination of syllables, expressing life, running, negative, and for females, a female or mother, negative. Thus in various permutations LR, LRN, LN, LNN, RN, RNN, LM, LRM, RM. In the Agaw, etc., is BR.

Mr. Tylor ("Early History," p. 312) quotes Humboldt, ("Vue des Cordilleras," pl. xv,) with regard to the Mexicans having retained the traditions of the elephant as a myth of observation. It has appeared to me that the Tasmanian names given to European animals resemble Sandeh names of African animals, which must have been preserved by tradition.

A good example of the common distribution of animal names will be found in those of the Nile region, Agaw, etc., with Guarani of Brazil, as Ta-piyra, Taia, etc.

The connection of the names of *Weapons*, with their distribution, was illustrated by me in a note on the words for arrow, in a paper on the Prehistoric Names for Weapons read at the British Association in 1873.

It was this investigation of the connection between archæology and philology, suggested by Colonel Lane Fox's lectures, which enabled me to lay a firmer basis for the investigation of the connections between India and Africa and between the new world and the old, because it became evident that these were prehistoric, and connected with successive migrations.

The names for weapons will of course vary in neighbouring tribes and be unequally distributed, and more particularly because the names of weapons are sometimes taken from conquering races.

It appears to me that the names BK, BN, and KN are formed on negative roots, as the word to kill or die, expressive of the characteristic of a weapon of death.

I shall now give some examples of the distribution of roots for arrow or dart, knife, sword, axe or hatchet, and spear or lance.

ROOT BK.

	Asia.	Africa.	South America.
Arrow	Gyarung—kipi Kari Naga—takaba Mru or Toung of Burmah—quai	... Houssa—kebia	... Itenes—kivo
Knife.		Houssa—takobi Fulah—kafahi Wolof—paku	... Skwali—khawughkhan ... Watlala ... (Chinook)—khawukhe Pujuni—kiai

	Asia.	Africa.	South America.
Sword		Houssa—takobi	
		Fulah—kafahi	
Spear.		Batta—kubi	

A curious point is in the parallel forms.

India—kipi ...	... Houssa—kebia
takaba ...	takobi

ROOT BN.

Arrow	Burmese—pen	... Mandingo—benyo
	Malay	... Bambarra—bien
	Javanese—pana	... Ashantee—eben
	Sanskrit—banah	
Knife.	Khond—penju	
	Telugu—banamu	
Spear.		Mandingo—benyo

ROOT KN.

Arrow	Tharu—khando	... Fanti—egandua
	Madi—kani	
	Chentsu—kondu	
	Tamil—kanei	

ROOT DM.

Arrow	Sontali—jhampa		Keracares—tomete
	Thaksya—tume		
	Tamil—ambu		
Spear.		Mandingo—tambu	
		Bambarra—tama	
		Ashantee—kami	
Axe ...		Ashantee—ekuma	

The bead in the Wolof and Vasco-Kolarian is related to egg, pea, bean. Thus it would appear as if beads were strung eggs and round seeds of plants. It may be that the pea and bean, being eatable, are named after egg and fowl, and that the bean was consequently endowed with various mythological attributes.

In Basque, the names for pea, bean, and acorn appear to be related to stone.

Mill was related to stone and rub.

Several names of weapons appear to be related to snake and dog, as if running swiftly, and endowed with life, others, as said, to death.

The phenomena of the PRONOUNS of a class are remarkable. In the early epochs they are seldom generally or evenly distributed. The first pronoun singular may be uniform, but even this is not a rule. The second and third persons are frequently interchanged.

It is, however, on pronominal and grammatical forms that many philologists most insist as a test of affinity.

A curious example of disturbance is found in Akkad and Georgian. Each has double plurals for nouns, for these in Georgian *bi* and *ni* are in Akkad the third personal pronoun.

The cause of this phenomenon is to be found, and is in fact

generally indicated in that excellent treatise on gesture language, which forms a chapter of the "Early History of Mankind." It is because gesture was used to determine the word used for a person as a pronoun.

The use of DETERMINATIVES for the distinction of classes of objects is inherent in the prehistoric languages. It is particularly applied to the members of the body, and sometimes to animals.

Its application will be sufficiently exhibited by its copious forms in Basque.

Comparative philology.—Prehistoric determinative or distinctive particles.

			Basque.					Basque.
Head	...	...	bu	Forehead	...	...	...	be
Hair	...	...	bi	Beard	...	...	...	bi
Eye	...	...	be, bel	Back	...	...	...	bi
Eyebrow	...	...	be, buff, bier	Breast	...	...	...	bul
Ear	...	...	be	Fowl	...	...	...	be
Head	...	...	bi	Cow ...	...	...	...	be ?
Arm	...	...	be	Grass (hair)	...	...	be, bel
Knee	...	...	be	Crow	...	...	...	be
Elbow ...	...	...	be	Mare	...	...	...	be
Nail finger	...	...	be	Lungs	...	...	...	bul
Thumb	...	...	be, ber	Tail ...	...	...	...	bu

The Coptic definite articles are:—Masculine, P-, Pi-; feminine, T-, Tii-, Te-; plural, Ne-, Nen-. These are probably derived from the older determinatives:—Vasco-Kolarian B-, Guarana-Agaw, T-, Te. The common prehistoric determinative:—N-, Ni-.

Animal members are marked out by O— North America:—Blackfoot, Cayuga, Mohawk, Onondaga, Tuscarora, Cahuilo.

What Mr. Tylor ("Primitive Culture," i, 220), has pointed out with regard to the DIFFERENCING of distance by sounds, in the case of pronouns and adverbs, and what Professor Max Müller, expounding various authorities, has shown with regard to gender, are only applications of a general law.

It is by differencing by vowels or consonants that in the prehistoric languages distinctions are drawn between the meanings of the same roots, and this is well seen in the way in which an animal name for dog is made distinctive for various animals.

This law of differencing has not received the attention it deserves. It is the true cause of some of the phenomena which have been attributed to normal changes of sounds, to phonetic laws, to Grimm's law in particular, and to phonetic decay, and as to which doctrines, Professor Max Müller has begun to show caution and to enforce it.

It is in what I term the NEGATIVE SERIES that one of the leading laws of prehistoric philology and mythology is to be found.

Under this, the negative no or not is the equivalent of night and black (Niger).

It is also the equivalent of woman, as the negative, man being treated as the positive. So all female names become negative, as wife, Eve, ewe, hound (=bitch), she-goat, cow, mare, etc.

[In another relation, woman becomes the equivalent of the Yona and mouth, and by her periodicity, resembling that of the moon, the equivalent of that body.]

Death, kill, executioner, have negative relations.

So have egg and nit, and secondarily pea, bean, and nut (as resembling an egg). Ear and head appear to be negative.

Cloud is a negative, and that is why, in modern verbal mythology or solar myths, it is found to conform with cow, as it may conform with any negative or female negative. Nephele, in mythology, is one of the forms of Khaveh or Eve.

Shadow is a negative, and in some cases equivalent to soul and night.

In Guarani, there is an ingenious distinction between the soul of the living and the dead; and so of a head, bone, skin.

The soul of the dead man is supposed in many countries to lodge in birds.

This may be one ground why the bird is negative as bearing the soul of the dead.

Blood is a negative apparently as related to death.

Hence red is a negative, and some curious mythological and archæological conditions arise, for red is likewise the equivalent of the number two.

Dr. Zerffy informs me that red was the second colour in various positions, as on dice, and on temple terraces, but this requires closer investigation.

Mr. Park Harrison and Mr. Jeremiah, jun., have observed the use of red as a colour widely prevalent in the regions now under consideration for the purposes of this investigation.

The virtue of red as a preservative against the evil eye is referred to in Walter K. Kelly's "Curiosities of Indo-European Traditions and Folk-lore" (p. 147). In Buchan, Aberdeenshire, the housewives tie a piece of red worsted round their cows' tails before turning them out to grass for the first time in spring. It is, however, better shown in Germany (p. 229), where herdsmen lay a woman's red apron, or a broad axe covered with a woman's red stocking, before the threshold of the cow-house, and make the animals step over it. The bringing together of woman, cow, and red is noteworthy.

The lady-bird seems to hold its place in folk-lore as being red (p. 95). It is held unlucky to kill a lady-bird in Germany, as the sun would not shine the next day.

It is possible that the robin redbreast owes his mythical place to the same characteristic, and it is also unlucky to kill him.

The woodpecker has a red head or mutch (p. 86) and a black body.

Bad is negative, as is naked.

Sleep and dream are negatives, as belonging to the night series.

Salt is negative.

Water in some senses is a negative, and appears to be connected with woman.

Night was the negative of day on the closing of the eye, and it had its own world of darkness, with its night sun, its sleep and its dreams. It was the domain of shadows and the ultimate refuge of the soul. Its mythological relations in this respect will best be studied in the treatment of animism by Mr. Tylor.

There are few prehistoric, protohistoric, or historic languages which do not display the Negative Series. Among such may be named : — Wolof, Agaw, Vasco-Kolarian (very marked), Ugrian, Egyptian, Sumerian (very marked), Dravidian, Semitic (not strongly marked), Aryan (very marked).

For Aryan, a popular illustration is afforded by Not, Night, Nut, Nit, Naked, Nest, Snow, Eve, Ewe, Egg, Wife, Cow, Nox, Nix, Nex, Nux, Nec, Non, Nudus, Nidus, Nodus, Niger, Nubes, Ovis, Ovum, Avis, Uva, Caput, Auris.

The way in which the negative roots are distributed among the various branches of a class is peculiar and affords a distinction.

Thus, Latin uses N largely, and O (KR) sparingly; Greek, M, O largely, and KR or KL sparingly. Thus Aymara uses P, K, H; Mon uses P (sparingly), K, H (sparingly) and T.

In reality the dissylables are chiefly the same, for the O (ovum, oon(is nothing but the K, B and KB of the Vasco-Kolarian, and Sumerian Gaba, Paka, and the KR (Karua, Auris, etc.) that of the Sumerian Raka.

The words for woman as Khaveh, Eve, Agave, Hebe, Nephele, Wife, have descended through ages as the formula for verbal mythology, and hence figure so largely in the earliest records of Genesis, in the traditions of the Eastern Mediterranean, and among the Aryans.

A sufficient example will be afforded by the following :—

NEGATIVE SERIES.

		Aymara.		Mon of Pegu.
Moon	ab	paksi	b	khatu
Red	ab	pako	ab	hpakit
Two	a	pa, paya	a	pa
Ear	ab	(paoki)	b	khato
Head	ab	phekai	b	katau

NEGATIVE SERIES—continued.

	Aymara.		Mon of Pegu.	
Night	bc	haipu	b	khatan
River	c	hahuiri	a	pi
No, not	c	hani	c	ha
Salt	o	hayu	a	po
Bad			bc	hakha
Bitter	c	haru	b	katan
Black	b?	chamaka?	b	katsau

The chief negative monosyllabic particles are M (Ma) and N (Na, No), and I differ from Mr. Tylor ("Primitive Culture," i, 19) as to their origin being interjectional; and from De Brosses, vol. i, p. 203; and Wedgewood, quoted by Tylor, as to N being a nasal interjection of doubt or dissent.

It appears reasonable to regard them under the new view as being in relation to the Ma or Na forms for mother, when these had been so distributed and applied. Mother being related to woman, stands in a negative condition.

The dissyllable form is largely developed with the negative.

It should be mentioned that a negative is not necessarily a prefix or suffix, but in prehistoric grammar may be intercalated, as in Gondi (Khond), Vasco-Kolarian, and Sumerian Akkad.

It is on this principle, probably, that in many languages we employ a middle negative, with negative verbs, as in Akkad, Turkish, etc., and with auxiliaries in our own and many modern languages.

In Chinese, Pe, which is elsewhere negative and black, means white; and it is possible that in some cases negatives have been made positives to propitiate a good omen.

GENDER is closely connected with the negative relations.

Mr. Tylor has very well said ("Primitive Culture," i, 301) that "the distinction of grammatical gender is a process intimately connected with the formation of myths." In addition to the explanations he has given, account should be taken of the effect of positive and negative ideas in gender.

I concur with him that the gender beyond the masculine and feminine is relatively modern, but this in many cases belongs to the trinary epoch, and is not in its origin a neuter gender, but a common gender.

It is possible that "the high caste or major gender," of Dravidian, including gods and men (Caldwell, Comp. Grammar, p. 172, quoted as above), may be connected with the same phenomena, because the common gender would be that of the chief god.

It is a matter of great question whether, so far as the prehistoric epoch is concerned, the supposed solar and lunar mythology can be effectually applied as an exponent, any more than it can under proper considerations to modern conditions. The verbal and mythological relation, in the prehistoric epoch, of women to the moon, for instance, is not properly a part of the modern meteorological mythology.

Upon the subject of NUMERALS, there is not the space to enlarge. If numerals are not always characteristic, because they are propagated and borrowed as instruments of culture, they are sometimes very valuable in that respect, as in the case of Akkad, Mon, and Peruvian. There is also much to be investigated as to their structure, other than in the course of the prevalent doctrines.

It has long since been pointed out that the word for man largely constitutes the TRIBAL NAME. Thus we have it in Aro, Ho, Aino, Mru, Minipo, Kuri, Kami, Kumi, Agoo, Singpho.

Black is the meaning of Wolof and Landoma.

Sun appears to be the name for Batta, Apach, Shan, Hayu, Fulah.

Many tribal names are widely distributed. The Mundara and others of Central India appear to be repeated in Central Africa.

The following is a list of some common names:

Asia.	Akush.	Kush.	Africa.
Asia ...	... Akhaioi ...	... Om-agua, etc.	... South America
Africa...	... Agaw	...	
Asia ...	... Sumer (Akkad)	... Aymara ...	... South America
„ ...	... Khmer Kemer (Cambodia ...	... Quichua...	... South America
„ ...	... Kissü (Babylonia)	... Quiche? ...	... Central America
Africa...	... Batta	... Batta ...	... Australasia (Sumatra)
India ...	... Bodo	... Abatia ? ...	... West Africa
„ ...	... Garo	... Yangaro...	... North Africa
East Nepaul...	... Magar... ...	... Magyar ...	... Europe
East Nepaul...	... Khun	... Hun ...	... Europe

The comparative mythology requires to be carefully studied on these facts and principles. The distribution of the names for sun, moon, and stars present peculiarities, some of which can be recognised in the old world.

The same type sometimes supplies sun, fire, and day.

A form for moon, largely found in North America, is night sun.

It is from this practice that we may account for the same word occasionally figuring for sun and moon without a distinctive. The male moon had perhaps a relation to the moon appearing during the day.

That eye has been used for sun, as in Indo-China and Australasia we find by Algonkin, Quichua, and Aymara.

Among the Salivi of the Orinoco we find for sun, sky-man; and among the Betoi of the Orinoco for sun, sky-man, and for moon, sky-woman.

Sky-man is possibly found in the Serpa of Thibet in the Singpho, Koreng, Khoibu, Mareng and Laos of the Burmese peninsula.

Having referred to the connection between the new world and the old, which is established by that great department of culture, speech, it would be desirable to deal with race, but that must be left for further examination. · Certainly the Esquimaux must be acknowledged, and there are many who will accept the principle of Humboldt that the Mongol type may be recognised in America. To me it appears that in the south, and also in the north, types may be seen that are common to Indo-China, India, and Africa. My study, however, is for the time being that of culture, and not that of the body.

The hair, so much regarded by some as a distinctive, has in America old world representatives.

With regard to skulls I can offer no opinion. That must be left to Professor Busk and his colleagues. At the same time, in this and in other inquiries we shall very probably find a difficulty the distinguished president of the Anthropological Institute has pointed out, and which now impedes the progress of craniology, and that is the want of distinctive characters in skulls of mixed races. In this we shall, however, most likely be ultimately assisted by the progress of other departments of anthropology. At present, even the finding together of long and short skulls affords little valuable material for determination.

The compression of skulls is, as Professor Busk remarks, a phenomenon to be observed around the shores of South America, but it is worth noting that it occurred in Peru and also in the hill parts of Pegu. (Prichard on "Man," iv, 537.)

The whole subject of skull deformities, in reference to America, will be found in Daniel Wilson's " Prehistoric Man," second edition, p. 491, and that of Peru in a paper by him in "Nature," May 21st, 1874, and which was a subject of controversy. It thence appears that such deformities are not peculiar to America, nor characteristic thereof, neither are they characteristic of the Agaw or Sumerian races, but they are worth studying, as they may ultimately furnish evidence.

Mr. Park Harrison refers to the extension of circumcision to Easter Island and Peru. It is distinctly observable in sculptures from Easter Island. Of its eastern extension it is unnecessary to speak.

Circumcision may possibly have some connection with the myth, recorded by Mr. Tylor ("Primitive Culture," i, 334), that in Brazil after a couple have been married, the father or father-in-law cuts a wooden stick with a sharp flint, imagining that by this ceremony he cuts off the tails of any future grandchildren, so that they may be born tailless. It will be observed that a circumcising instrument is used, a sharp flint.

Mr. J. Park Harrison, who, as stated, has devoted much attention to the various ethnological phenomena connecting the west and the east, has treated among others of the artificial enlargement of the earlobe among various nations, in the Journal of the Anthropological Institute, July and October, 1872, p. 190. Cases of this kind are prominent enough among the Indo-Chinese.

Consul Hutchinson ("Peru," vol. i, p. 138 and 139) pointedly refers to an example in a little wooden idol from the Cerro del Oro, and he found others in the museum at Lima (vol. i, p. 321). In Mr. John L. Stephens' "Central America", vol. i, examples may be found at pages 139, 143, 149, 150, 152, 153, and 158. David Forbes refers (p. 41) to the love for great ear ornaments among the Aymaras. It is stated that the Incas only granted permission to indulge in enlarged ear-lobes as a privilege to the Aymaras a long time after their annexation to the empire.

The question of mound monuments is one that must be passed over as one not coming into the epoch we are now engaged with.

In Polynesia the remains of massive stone buildings have been found in Tongatabu, Easter Island, Rota, Tinian, Valan, and elsewhere (Wilson's "Prehistoric Man," p. 109). To these may be added Java, Pegu, Cambodia, Peru, Mexico, and Yucatan.

Among the facts adduced by Mr. Park Harrison for the migration from east to west through Australasia he refers to colossal heads in the east and in Easter Island. Colossal heads will be found in Stephens' "Central America, Chiapas, and Yucatan, vol. i, p. 139, 143, 149, 150, 152, 153 and 328. They have been identified in Babylonia, Cambodia, Easter Island, and Peru.

M. Perrot, under the name of Lydo-Phrygian, and myself, under the name of Lydo-Assyrian, have pointed out the westerly extension of the monuments in Asia Minor, including the Niobe near Magnesia ad Mœandrum and the Pseudo Sesostris, near Nymphæ in the Smyrna district. To this may be added the colossal head from the outskirts of Smyrna, found by Mr. F. Spiegelthal, in 1865, and identified by me and brought to the British Museum by Mr. G. Dennis. The name of Lydo-Akkadian is perhaps better for these monuments.

The use of enormous blocks of admirably squared stone, without cement, is a feature common to both continents and deserving of investigation, as well as the mode in which such blocks were quarried and transported. In South America there were no beasts of burthen available. The employment of bricks and cement, and generally the adoption of the building arts are also worthy of careful examination.

Stephens, in his "Yucatan," vol. i, p. 134, gives a very remarkable engraving of a capital of a column at Uxmal, of old world character.

At Uxmal there are buildings constructed on terraces and mounds, as there were at Babylon (i, 135). This is worth observing for further comment.

Burial towers are to be recognised in Syria, Persia, India, Siam, and Peru.

The knowledge of bronze, goldsmith's work, silver work, and other metallurgy has not passed unobserved by writers. Gold dentistry has been recognised in Peru and Egypt (Tylor, "Early History of Mankind," p. 175).

The employment of bronze in America presents no difficulty under the acceptation of a Sumerian settlement. If the Agaws did not become acquainted with the large tin supplies of Malacca the East Sumerians did, as they were with the working of gold and silver. Hence they readily introduced these arts into America, or rather improved them, because the mound builders were acquainted with copper and bronze working.

Although the Sumerians, as the topographical nomenclature shows, were acquainted with tin in Britain before the Phœnicians, it is probable Malacca, and not Britain, was the great seat of the early supply of tin.

Consul Hutchinson ("Peru," ii, 266) institutes a justifiable comparison between the masonry and pottery of ancient Peru, observed by himself, and the prehistoric discoveries of Dr. Schliemann in the Troad. In fact, if my views are correct of the connection of the Lydians, Phrygians, and Carians of Asia Minor, with the Etruscans and the Sumerians, then there would be a positive identification of epoch and class between the Troad and Peru.

In Peru, drinking cups and other articles were buried with the dead, as in Etruria, etc. The Peruvian cups were supposed to be used for drinking at the funerals (Forbes, 49).

The woven fabrics are also to be noted in connection with Peru and the country of the Thinæ or Cambodia.

The quipu or knotted cord, as a record, is found in Peru, Mexico, Hawaii, Polynesia, the Eastern Archipelago, and China (Prichard, iv, 466 ; Tylor, "Early History of Mankind, pp. 156, 160).

The scape llama referred to by David Forbes (p. 45) may be compared with the scape goat of the east.

Sacrifices of men to the gods were used by the earlier races, as the Dahomans, but it is to be noted that they were a practice

D

also of the worship of Baal, in Peru and in Mexico (Wilson, "Prehistoric Man," pp. 89, 91, 290), as also in the east.

Von Humboldt long since noticed the connection of the Mexican calendar with the Asiatic and deduced the Asiatic origin of the civilization (see also E. B. Tylor, "Anahuac," 241). The Yucatan calendar is allied to the Mexican. The subject of the calendars and inscriptions, together with Peruvian and Central American languages has long occupied the Chevalier Bollaert, the author of the Peruvian antiquities and of many memoirs, particularly on the Maya alphabet.

The half month in the early Maya or Yucatan calendar consisted of thirteen days (Stephens' "Yucatan", i, 439). The Siamese likewise use as an essential part of a date a half month. This now consists of fourteen days.

The dates in Siamese are arranged on a cross (+). In Yucatan, part of the cycle was placed on a wheel divided into four, practically N, E, W, and S. The two systems show a resemblance, and the cross may represent the spokes of a wheel. The Yucatan calendar, which was the same as the Mexican, has lucky and unlucky days, still a common system in the east. The cross has been found by Dr. Schlemann in the Troad. The square cross is common among the Aymaras (Forbes, 39), and was observed by Stephens in Central America.

The red hand seen in the monuments of Yucatan (Stevens) Bollaert says he has seen as far south as Arica in Peru ("Anthropology of the New World," 114).

Chewing vegetable substances, so well known in the east, takes place in Peru with coca. David Forbes also observes that besides eating clay the Aymaras and Quichuas mix ashes of wood on plants with the coca leaf, and that this is like the Asiatic practice of adding lime to the betel nut, being in both cases for the purpose of setting free the vegetable alkaloid of the plant (p. 59). The coca was anciently offered on the altar of the gods, and now on the altar of the Virgin.

The Honourable Mr. Clay points out that the umbrella was a mark of dignity among the Peruvians, as it was in Babylonia, and is still in the Indo-Chinese countries.

PART II.

The Connection of Culture in Asia and America.

The affinities of grammar between the new world and the old, though dealt with by various writers, as in the "Mithridates," were only scientifically treated by a few, as by Humboldt, the Rev. Richard Garnett, and Dr. Daniel Wilson ("Prehistoric

Man," p. 594). Characters common to the Polynesian had been recognised, but Mr. Garnet pointed out that besides these others were to be found common to the languages of the Dekkan in India.

On the other hand, Dr. Oscar Peschel, in his " Volkerkunde," 1874, p. 472, still maintains that the culture of Peru and Mexico was indigenous.

Mr. Tylor also ("Early History of Mankind," p. 209) says " No certain proof of connection or intercourse of any kind between Mexico and Peru seems as yet to have been made out." This expresses the state of prevalent opinion, and although the materials for linguistic investigation are abundantly displayed in Dr. Latham's valuable "Elements of Comparative Philology," such opinion has been little contested. In fact, although the languages are allied, yet that alliance has to be demonstrated from the outside, and until the disinterment and decipherment of the Sumerian or Akkad inscriptions, it was almost impossible to be proved.

The Aymara and Quichua languages of Peru, the Aztek of Mexico, and the Maya of Yucatan, are all allied with the Indo-Chinese, and thereby with the Akkad as Sumerian. Even to the Negative Series and numerals the points of resemblance are remarkable. Some of these resemblances between Akkad and Quichua had, on the perusal of M. Lenorment's works, struck Señor de la Rosa, a distinguished Peruvian scholar, and on the reading of this paper at the Anthropological Institute he referred to several examples lying on the surface. He also referred to resemblances between Quichua and Semitic and Aryan. These I treated as resulting from the influence of Sumerian and the older languages, as Semitic and Sanskrit.

In Peru and Bolivia the chief languages now are the Quichua or Inca, and the Aymara.

Of the AYMARA a copious and valuable memoir was, on 21st June, 1870, communicated to the Ethnological Society (parent of the Anthropological Institute) by David Forbes, F.R.S., and this constitutes a text-book.

The language of the Aymaras is spoken in southern Peru and northern Bolivia. They were conquered by the Incas. The Quichua is spoken in northern Peru and southern Bolivia.

The Aymaras claim to have been a great people before the Inca conquest (1100), perhaps beyond any South American people. Ruins of grand palaces and temples remain at Tiahuanaca on the south of Lake Titicaca (Forbes). Tiahuanaca was the capital of the Aymara land. The conquest of it was completed in 1289, but was followed by serious revolts.

Forbes says, too, (p. 4) that, according to Indian traditions from Aymara as well as Quichua sources, the Aymaras, even before the time of the first Inca, Manco—Capac (1021-1062)—possessed a degree of civilisation higher than that of the Incas themselves. Consul Hutchinson maintained before the Institute a like doctrine as to the Chimoos.

The Aymara is related to the Quichua, which was the governmental language of Peru under the Incas. Among people devoted to the worship of the Sun it might be expected the word for Sun would be remarkable, but so it is only in one respect, that the word Inti is the word for Eye in the African Danakil. It is one canon in prehistoric philology that Eye and Sun are permutable, because the Sun was called the Sky-eye.

The Aymara, etc., resemblances to Danakil, Shiho, and Adaiel of North-east Africa are thus shown :—

		Peru.				Danakil, etc.
Eye ...	... naira—Aymara	...	... Sun ...	... aero
Sun ...	... inti ,,	...	... Eye ...	... inti
Head	... uma, homa ,,	...	... Head	... ammo
Nose	... cenca, cinga Q	...	... Nose	... san
Ear ...	... paoki	...	...	... Ear ...	... okua
Star ...	... silla...	...	...	... Moon	... alsa
Day ...	... uru ...	...	...	... Day ...	... erra

The eye of the Aymara, says Forbes (p. 14), has the central line very slightly inclined inwards, not nearly so much as in the Mongol, yet not altogether horizontal as in many of the Chinese. An approximation to this form of eye is observable among the Indo-Chinese, but then it must be noted that it is also found among the Guaranis of Brazil.

Forbes (p. 12) says, that " the figure given in ' Smith's Natural History of the Human Species ' of an Indian of the Otto tribe in North America is almost an exact likeness of Conduri, an old Aymara man some time in my service."

Although Tschudi attributes the elongated skulls to the Incas, it was, as Forbes points out (p. 13), to the Aymaras that belonged the skulls found near Lake Titicaca. The Aymara language is nearest to the Peguan, and it is in Arakan, near the Peguan area, that among hill tribes the system of flattening the skull is now practised. (Prichard on " Man," Vol. iv. p. 537).

With regard to the hair of the Aymaras, it is extremely abundant and long in the man as well as the woman. It is of a deep black-brown or black colour, perfectly straight, without any attempt to curl (Forbes, p. 14). It is noticeable that the men wear their hair drawn backwards over their heads, and plaited into a long pigtail. This practice corresponds with that of Asia. Forbes notes that the women have two pigtails. This appears recognisable on Etruscan and some archaic monuments of the west. The men are proud of their pigtails, and Forbes believes introduce false hair. This is done in China. Cutting off the pigtail is as there the severest punishment (p. 44).

The Aymara and Quichua Indians are noted for their character of submission to authority, enabling them to be used for the foundation of a great empire, and this is a feature of the Indo-Chinese people.

The Aymara area has been supposed to be limited to that now occupied, but it is to be observed that the names found in the neighbourhood of Lake Titicaca are much better developed in New Granada. It is therefore evident that the Aymara, or perhaps pre-Aymara, occupation must have extended so far north. Mr. Clements Markham considers that the Inca empire never reached so far northward, and Mr. Forbes was not aware of such an extension of the Aymara as must now be allowed for.

Aymara is possibly the equivalent of Kemer or Khmer, the name of the Cambodians, and of the Sumer—the name of the people connected with Accad.

QUICHUA in Peru and Quiché in Mexico may represent the Kissii or Cissii near Babylon; and these may be connected with Cush and Akush. Of the Quichua or Inca language and people it is not necessary to say so much, as they are more familiarly known, and have been and will be incidentally referred to.

To the Quichua language Mr. Clements Markham has devoted himself, and produced a grammar and dictionary which have been of very great service in these investigations. I have also employed the Arte of Torres Rubio, on which his grammar is founded. This work of Mr. Markham's is likely to be of more importance even than he anticipated now that Quichua and Aymara must be studied for the comparative grammar of Akkad. Señor de la Rosa and Señor Pacheco are engaged on new Quichua Grammars.

Consul Hutchinson, who has given so much labour to the prehistoric archeology of Peru, places the CHIMOOS before the Quichuas in Peru; but I have no specimen of the language.

The AZTEK culture of Mexico, as Humboldt well saw, was derived from the old world, as was its language, which is to be classed with Sumerian, but intermediate between Aymara and Otomi.

The Otomi, Cora, and Tarahumars, with perhaps the Huastcca, constitute a class under Sumerian influence, but allied with the Adighe or Circassian, which likewise exhibits Sumerian influence, and has a remarkable but distant resemblance with Etruscan.

In the Circassian I had long since traced what are called North American characteristics, and others I found in the Georgian, but the cause was unknown to me till of late. A considerable influence must have been exerted by the Agaw and Otomi migrations on the Indian languages of North America.

The presence of the Circassian-Otomi has to be accounted for. The higher Sumerians are marked as city-building people, but the Circassian in the Caucasus is what the Otomi is in Mexico. The Otomis must have preceded the Sumerians in South America or been driven forward by them, as the Agaw-Guarani were into Brazil. The Otomis may have had connections or dealings with the monument-building races of North America. At a later date, on the Sumerian kingdoms in Mexico becoming weaker, they returned and invaded Mexico.

Dr. Latham ("Opuscula, Essays," 1860, p. 395) gives "the result of a very hurried collation," for the Otomi, "said to be "with the languages akin to the Chinese *en masse*" (p. 397), and for the Maya (p. 398). The latter list is chiefly of Aztek words. He makes no remarks, but the tables show many affinities with Tonkin and Cochin-Chinese. Had Dr. Latham followed this up he might probably have obtained the clue to the relation of the Mexican languages, though he might have been baffled, as some of the affinities can only be illustrated by bringing together the Quichua and Aymara as members of the group, and the Akkad then undeciphered. It is, in fact, now a part of the evidence that Humboldt, Garnett, Latham, etc., are found to have contributed material for the true solution.

The history of Mexico is supplied from accessible sources. Its best known language is the Aztek. On the preceding Toltek I can throw no light. The monuments and culture of Mexico may, after the reference already made to them, be passed over. Suffice it to say, the monuments are of great dimensions and highly decorated.

Yucatan possesses similar remains described by J. L. Stephens. The MAYA, a language formerly cultivated, comes distinctly within the Sumerian class.

In "Incidents of Travel," by J. L. Stephens, in Central America, Chiapas and Yucatan, in vol. ii, are hieroglyphics, which are arranged in rows, and appear to present some of the principles of the cuneiform or hieratic, as ||| |! ||| ||||
☐ ||

The same is to be observed at Palenque, ii, 342 and 424. These latter present even more resemblance to the Hamath inscriptions, as ☉ ◎, also the extended arm (see also Hissarlik and Easter Island) is worth further examination.

The square hieroglyphics, or rather squares of hieroglyphics, found in Central America, are most probably only a modification of the row or column of hieroglyphics in the Yucatan and Hamath, and which has a representative in hieratic cuneiform. The carvings on the rocks at the Yonan Pass, in Peru, engraved by Consul T. J. Hutchinson ("Peru," ii, 174, 176), are deserving of study. Some of the characters are ideographs, but some likewise present a resemblance to Hamath and other characters ; and Easter Island inscriptions deserve attention.

The question may be incidentally considered whether the Sumerian population of Indo-China was supplied from Babylonia or the common centre in High Asia. In my view it was from the common centre, because although there are great affinities between Sumerian or Akkad and its eastern analogues, yet there are greater affinities between these, and there are common points of dissimilarity from Sumerian. There were most probably two migrations of Sumerian in succession to the Agaw. One embraced the Akkad, Mon, Cambodian, Aymara, and Maya (and Toltec ?). The other, the Georgian, Etruscan, Siamese, Quichua, and Aztek. The earliest may, however, have been the Circassian Otomi.

Mr. Park Harrison strongly maintains that civilisation must have had a passage from the Old World to Peru by Easter Island, and he has brought the subject before the Anthropological Institute and the British Association. The phenomena here described of the distribution of population in South America greatly favour this view. There were, however, looking to geographical circumstances, probably two routes by the northern and southern islands and currents, and these may have effected the collocation of the various populations.

Proceeding onwards, INDO-CHINA, or the southern districts of the further peninsula beyond India, may be treated as one linguistic area. They include Pegu in the west, Siam in the middle, and Cambodia in the east. This region was known to the ancients as being held by populations in a state of advancement.

Pegu is the country at the mouth of the Irawaddy, and was formerly independent, but fell under the dominion of the Burmese empire. In 1852, the province, with the towns of Pegu, Prome, and Rangoon was taken by the English. The people call themselves Mon, but are called Talaïn by the Burmese. The language is a most valuable member of the Sumerian for illustration. There are large ruins.

Siam lies in the middle of India, beyond the Ganges, and is the seat of a great and settled empire. The Siamese people and language are, however, of less importance to us in this inquiry at this period than are the others.

Kambodia, or Camboja (Kan-phu-cha, Chinese), is the western part of Annam or Cochin-China on the Saïgong and Kambodia rivers, borders on eastern Siam. Of late years it has been attacked by the French, who have taken and hold Saïgong.

The great marble ruins of the ancient capital of the Thinæ, near Saïgong have long been known. The Kambodians were remarked by the early Arab voyagers as manufacturers of very fine linen. The natives call themselves Kammeren Khmer (=Aymara). Kitaya, too, or Indo-China, may be equivalent to Kissii, or Cissi, and to Quichua. It is to be observed that the explored monuments of Kambodia are not ancient like those of Babylonia, but rather modern and synchronous with those of Peru and Mexico, but it is probable earlier remains will be found.

Kambodia has been studied by M. Mouhot, by M. Garnier in his large and valuable work, and lately by Mr. Kennedy, in his paper read before the Indian Section of the Society of Arts (Journal, 1873-4), when I presided, and had the opportunity of giving some early explanations of the linguistic relations as recorded in the Journal of the Society.

The ancient kingdom of Camboja, in India, which gave name to the Gulf of Camboja, or Cambay, has engaged the attention of Indian archeologists, but not to the degree its importance merits. In the later history of this kingdom it was still considerable, but it was the representative of an ancient and perhaps the earliest civilisation of India, belonging to that epoch, which was universal, of which General Cunningham has found the examples.

The river names of India are repeated in New Granada on the one hand and in Etruria and Italy on the other, in conformity, as I stated in a note sent to the International Congress of Orientalists (N. Trübner). The town names obey the same law. It was from India and not from Babylonia that we may, as said, assume that the stream of civilisation passed towards the Pacific, and in India will yet be found the origins and remains of early letters, the influence of which to this day will still be recognised. The two names of the hundred-streamed feeder of the Indus, *Hes*udrus (100, Georgian), and *Zad*udrus (100, Sanskrit), are worthy of note as also *athasi* (1,000, Georgian), and *athasi* (88 Hindustani).

The Akkad, or Sumerian, must be looked upon as a main stock of the class. Of the cuneiform inscriptions, the Assyrian and the later Persian had been deciphered, while an early type, named after the kings of Accad, remained obscure. Mr. Oppert supported a non-Semitic and non-Aryan interpretation, and by the help of the Rev. A. H. Sayce and Mons. F. Lenormant, many of the characters have now been read, and the language is disclosed to the world.

What that language may be has been hitherto a matter of dispute. The chief authorities upon it have shown many relations with Vasco-Kolarian and Ugrian, while I have confirmed my own forecast ("Journal of the Anthropological Institute," 1871, pp. 53, 58) that it would be found to have Georgian affinities, and to belong to a Palæo-Asiatic class. I am now, however, able more distinctly to assign its position, by showing that, whatever its other affinities may be, it is closely connected in language with the former monument and city-building races of the Old and New World.

In the tenth chapter of Genesis, Accad is brought into the scheme of classification under the family of Ham. "The early kings of [Chaldea] entitled themselves rulers of Sumiri and Accad" (Sayce, "Journal of Philology," vol. iii, 1). Dr. Hincks, on the strength of inscriptions belonging to Accad, had proposed for the language the name of Accad, but Mr. Oppert directed attention to the fact that the people called themselves Sumir or Sumer, and urged the adoption of the term Sumerian. This appears worthy of support from the nature of allied forms. Samaria, a holy city and country, Semirus in Armenia, and Seumara in Iberia, are perhaps forms of Sumer. Raamah and Roma would be conformable. Armenia belongs to the same stock and epoch.

Smyrna (Smurna) and Samorna, of Ephesus, may also be assigned, as may be Asmurna of Hyrkania and Zimura of Aria. Ephesus and Smyrna must have been great seats of Sumerians. There we have Mount Sipylus (Sipula), with the Suburu or statue (Akkad) of Niobe. Near is another Lyde-Sumerian sculpture, the Pseudo-Sesostris of Nympha. Near Ephesus is Pygela or Pugela (Pucala, Pucara, the castle), the R changing to L in this district.

It is to be observed that, besides the cuneiform, wedge-shaped, or arrow-headed, there is an earlier character of the Akkad people, to which Mr. Oppert has given the name of "hieratic." In my opinion the Hamath inscriptions of Syria are to be deciphered on this basis, and the Maya of Yucatan has apparent resemblances. If this be the case we may look for inscriptions of the Akkad period, if not class, in the buried cities of India. It was long since pointed out by me that there were early alphabets, independent of Phœnician, and springing from the basis of the hieratic and arrow-headed, and I referred to ‖ being used in arrow-headed, and the Libyan of Thugga for Son, to the probable connection of ⊹, Hamath, ∗ hieratic, and א Hebrew, with Cypriate, and to other characters common in Warka, Cypriote, Himyaritic, and Albanian. The passage of an alphabet from Babylonia is now acknowledged through the discoveries in Cypriote and at Hissarlik. I attribute the Celtiberian characteristics to a like origin.

The GEORGIAN languages afford an interpretation of some of the terms of the pre-Hellenic topographical nomenclature of the Old World. These languages now include the Karthueli or Georgian, the Swan, the Lazian of Asia Minor, the Mingrelian, etc. One ancient representative appears to me to have been the Canaanite.

While the names of rivers and places are uniform in Asia Minor, the few remains of the language and inscriptions, except the Lycian, which is most likely Lesghian, appear to conform to a Canaanite or Georgian standard. To this, in compliance with ancient tradition, the Etruscan is by me annexed, as it was in 1870 and 1871 (" Journal of the Anthropological Institute," pp. 56, 58), although it must be stated that my materials of interpretation have as yet been scanty. The Rev. Isaac Taylor, who has published a book on a Ugrian hypothesis of Etruscan, at the Congress of Orientalists produced a further paper as to the connection of Etruscan with Accad, which is based upon and confirms my views. In illustration of the general connection, and of the interesting question of Etruscan, Tables I and II may be referred to.

One source of Etruscan, as of some other extinct languages, is to be traced by the same process of " survival " as in all anthropological departments. Latin will, when duly worked by analysis, form a rich mine.

SURVIVALS OF ETRUSCAN IN LATIN.

Goat ...	... capra	...	...	...	
Spring	... scaturigo	...	...	... tsqori, Georgian	
	scatebra, etc....	...	... tsqaroni	„
Sieve ...	... cribrum	...	...	... tskhrili	„
Old ...	... vetus	...	...	... azvili	„
Straw, pipe	... stipula	...	...	... thskepli	„
Seat ...	... scabellum	...	...	...	
	scamnus	...	...	...	
Crime ...	... scelus	...	...	... tsodva	„
Brush ...	... scopetus	...	...	... tsetskhi	„

While Canaanitic and Hamath come within the Hamitic scheme of Genesis, and are so far allied to Sumerian, which their character of culture supports ("Journal of the Anthropological Institute," 1871, p. 58), yet there are divergences of language and of culture so great that I cannot but regard the Canaanitic, Lydian, and Etruscan, as constituting a distinct

TABLE I.

	Etruscan.	Georgian.	Others.	America.
Boy, son	agalletor	shwili (akhali, young)	chvalay, Circas	akun, Mexican
	maris	krma	bosheth, Canaanite	butsi, Othomi
	puii?	bichi	—	
		boshi		
Goat	kapra	tkhavi	khapa, Mon	paka, Peruvian
Ape	arimus	[iremu, stag]		
Eagle	antar	arthsiri		
Hawk	aracus	kori (vulture)	—	kondori, Quichua, Peruvian
		archaqi (pelican)		
Beetle	burrus	buzi (fly)		
Swan	tusna	sawat		
Crane	grinis	ikvi (duck)		ancana, Quichua; eagle, Peruvian
Heaven	falandum	—	vouafay, Circas	andvui, Misteca
Apollo	usil	—	zal, Accad	sillo Aymara (star) Peruvian
Diana	tala		la, Burman	citlali, Aztek
				llantu, Peruvian
Ghost, shadow	hinthial	(nitheli, dark)		
Helmet	cassis	chachkani		
Black	thapir	shavi	shoouseh, Circas	
Brown	kiarthialisa	kardzi		
Strong	kahathial	—	atta, Circas, high	
I, me	me	mi	mu, Akkad	
And	cei	—		
Born	alisa	(shweli, child)		
Cupid	agfisur	qwar, love; shur, desire		qa, Quichua, Peruvian
Vulcan	sethlans	tsetskhli, fire		tleti, fire, Mexican
Make, work	kana	qana		kana cut, Aymara, Peruvian
Aurora	thesan	—	tuna, Akkad, dawn	

TABLE II.

	Etruscan.	Georgian.	Akkad.	Circas.	Camb.,etc.	Canaan.	Peruvian.
1...	makh	—	—	—	moe ...	—	mai
2...	thu	..: —	—	oh ...	—	—	yscay
3...	zal	... sami ... essa	... shee	... htsan	sam	... kimsa
4...	huth	... othkbi...	—	—	—	—	ttahua
5...	ki, kiem	... khuthi...	—	—	—	—	—
6...	sas	... ekusi ... as	... shoa	.. sau	...	—	sojta
7...	be(m)ph	... shwıdi...	—	—	—	—	pakalko
10...	alchl?	...	—	—	—	—	kalko

branch, at present to be assigned to Sumerian, but perhaps
afterwards to be sub-divided.

In the following illustrations the same characteristics as in
Etruscan are to be found :—

	Asia Minor.	W. and E. Asia.	America.
Earth	... gissa, Lydian	... yatta, Circas; Khsach, Cambodian]	
Water	... vedu, Phrygian	... pseh, Circas; pi, Mon labtayeh, Huastec	
Rock	... taba, Carian	... ——	tepe, Aztek
Garden	... ganos, Phrygian	... kana, Georgian; gana	
		Accad	
Village, town	.deba, Thracian	... daba, Georgian	... deba, Guarani
Fat, oil	... pikerion, Phrygian	pshey, Circas; pa?	
		Accad ...	... raccu, Quichua
Sheep	... ma, Phrygian	... maylley, Circas; me	
		(goat) Cambodian .. llama, Peruvian	
Horse	... ala, Carian	... [la, animal syllable,	
		Accad]	
King	... gala, Carian	... ungal, Accad	...

Hamath, or some such local metropolis, most likely afforded
the centre of a distinct development of civilisation, with trinal
forms of language and mythology, and producing syllabic and
alphabetic characters, afterwards attributed to the Phœnicians.

Georgian and Akkad have double plurals, the remains of a
prehistoric characteristic, and there are resemblances in the verbs
and numerals, but there are dissimilarities. As already written,
the Georgian double plurals -ni and -bi figure as third personal
pronouns in Akkad. These particles are not without resemblance
to negatives.

At an early period of the examination of Georgian, I was
much struck with the propensity for sticking in or inserting
consonants, as in Mexican and other languages. The immediate
explanation of the *tl* in Mexican is, however, to be sought in
Circassian. In Georgian it is perhaps *th.*

The exact affinities of Georgian are not shown by the existing
members of the Sumero-Peruvian class. Some are found in Ka,
a language allied to the Indo-Chinese group, and some in Cambodian. Georgian is evidently related to Etruscan. Thus—

Head ...	... thawi, Georgian	... tuwi, Ka
Mouth	... piri ...	... soar ,,
River ...	... mdinare ...	... daktani, Ka; tanle, Cambodian
Rock, mountain } Stone ... } tma		tamoe ,,

The elements of Georgian are found in the numerals 1 erthi, G (trao K); 2 ori (bur); 3 sami (tam); 4 othki (chin); 5 khouthi (ka); 8 rwa (peh); 9 tskhratsar (Khong).

Ka is found for 5 on the left-hand in Mon.

The Georgian numerals equal the left-hand Mon and Ka numerals.

COMPARISON OF AKKAD AND GEORGIAN GRAMMAR.

	Akkad.				Georgian.
=	Nouns more than one plural				
=	Emphatic form ending in a vowel				
=	Nagative series	...	...	...	...
=	Formation of persons of verbs				
=	Formation of participle				
=	Formation of negative verbs by the prefix Nu				
=	Resemblance of numbers ...	...	...	...	
=	Insertion in verb of pronouns governed		...	...	
=	Use of postpositions	...	...	...	...
=	Use of Ni, Bi ..	...	...	...	...	Na
=	Use of M and S				

The following tables show the comparison of Akkad :—

COMPARISON OF AKKAD AND QUICHUA GRAMMAR.

Akkad.	Quichua.
NOUN, emphatic state—a	None
,, Dual = 2 (kas)	Dual regarded = 2 (pura)
,, pronouns postportional =	
,, several plurals =	=
,, pl—ene =	-cuna -ntin
—mes	
,, plural by duplication =	
,, locative—ta =	-ta, through
,, ablative—na =	-nae, wanting
,, opportune—gal = ?	-ccepi (after, behind)
VERBS, governed	persons not the same
pronouns incorporated =	
,, plural—une—ne =	-un ?
—mus—s	-chic
,, gan to be, exist =	can, to be
Noun	numeral used without plural
Adjective after noun	before noun
Pronouns S. 1 ? 2 ? 3, two forms	
Pl. 3 =	
,, Demonstrative some resemble =	
Conjunction Cama, with, and =	cama, according as
Numerals, many =	all
ordinals—kam =	-nequen

Referring to affinities of language, the town of Eten in Peru is said to have a peculiar language, and it is asserted that the population can converse with the Chinese labourers. This statement has been quoted by Mr. Clements Markham, and is denied by Consul Hutchinson ("Peru," vol. ii, p. 202), who visited Eten. As the Consul does not give any Chinese, or any specimen of the language, it is difficult to decide. He quotes Mr. Stevenson as saying that they speak Chimoo. If this language is allied to the other cultivated languages of Peru, then some numerals and a few other words may resemble Chinese and give foundation for the report.

It will be seen that the resemblance to the Indo-Chinese is such as to give an explanation of many of the supposed cases of connection with Chinese. One of the best examples of supposed linguistic resemblance to Chinese was given by Mr. Stephen Powers in the "Atlantic Monthly" for March, 1874, p. 321, with regard to the Gallinomero. These are tribes on the north-west coast of America, near Healysburg, on the lower reaches of Russian River. The identification is, however, inconclusive, because Gallinomero is allied to Khwakhlamayu, and that again to Kulunapu, which again is a branch of the Yuma class. Mr. C. G. Leland has undertaken to publish an account of the Chinese intercourse with North America.

	Gallinomero.			Khwakhlamayo.		Chinese.
1...	... ehah	...	...	——		yih
2...	... ako	...	...	——		ar
3...	... sibbo	...	...	——		san
4...	... metah	...	...	——		se
5...	... shuh	...	...	——		wu
6...	... lancha	...	...	·——		luh
7...	... latko	...	...	——		tsih
8...	... kometah	...	...	——		pah
9...	... chapko	...	...	——		khi
10...	... chasuto	...	...	——		shih
Fire	... oho	...	...	——		sho
Dog	... hiyu	...	...	——		kinen
Day	... majih	...	...	——		jih
Eye	...	——		iiu	...	... yen
Mouth	...	——		aa	...	... hou
Hand	...	——		psha	...	... shen
Foot	...	——		sakhi	...	... kio
Wood, log	... moosu	...	...	——		muteu
Great	... bata(ta)	...	...	——		ta
Du, make	... tseena	...	...	——		tso
Sun	... ada	...	...	——		yat
Strength	... cha	...	...	——		chelih

The resemblance of the names of places is very deceptive, but that between the names of Peruvian and Yucatan places and Old World nomenclature is so striking as to require record, and it suitably follows the linguistic portion. In fact, there is scarcely a Peruvian or Maya name which cannot be at once dealt with; but Mexican is more refractory. The nomenclature of India within and beyond the Ganges, of Babylonia, of

Etruria, and Italy, and even of Britain, is reproduced or represented in South America.

The Rev. Mr. Sayce states (" Journal of Philology," 1870, vol. iii, p. 45) that "a continuation of W. Von Humboldt's researches in local names has extended the range of the Basque across the south of Europe as far as Asia Minor, and the sub-family thus formed may conveniently be called " Iberian." This is an error in which I have shared, as W. Von Humboldt includes many names in Spain as Basque which are not so, and the names so spoken of may be found in India or Peru.

The following shows the river names of New Granada in comparison with India and Italy (Etruria):—

New Granada.	India, etc.	Italy, etc.
Cane ...	...Cainas	...
Guayabera	... Chaberis	...
Guape ...	... Kophos	...
Cusiana ...	... Acesines ...	... Casuentus
Catarumbo	... Catabeda ...	...
Cibao ...	... ——	Gabellas
Garigoa ...	... Gouraios ...	...
Cauca ...	... Cacathis ...	... Caicus, A. Minor
Ite ...	... ——	Utis
Humedea ...	... Namadas ...	...
Lengupa ...	... ——	Longinus
Ariguani ...	... [Rhogomanus, Persia]	... Rigonum
Meta ...	... Andomatis ...	... Medoakus
Margua ...	... [Margus, Margiana]	... Nikia, Nato
Nachi ...	... ——	Nar, Nure
Nare ...	... ——	Anapus
Napipi ...	... ——	[Enipeus, Macedonia]
Neusa ...	... ——	Anassos
		[Nessos, Macedonia]
Upia ...	... ——	[Abus, Britain]
Paute ...	... Spauto, lake ...	... Padus
		[Bœtis, Spain]
Togui ...	... Tokosanna ...	... Togisonus
Tamar ...	... Tamarus ...	... Tamarus
	[Tamyrus, Syria] ...	... [Tamaros, Britain]
Tachira ...	... ——	Ticarios
Tiguanaqui	... ——	Digentia
Tumila ...	... Temala ...	...
Onzaga ...	... —	Sekies
Zulia ...	... —	Silis, Silarus
Suta ...	... Sadus	...
Sarare ...	... Serus	... Sarius
Suarez ...	... Sarabis ...	... Siris
		... Æsurus
Sisigua ...	... Suasius ...	... Sossius
Semindoco	... Tokosanna ...	...
Sumapia ...	... ——	Sumathus, Sicily
Sichiaca ...	... Sittokakis ...	... Sekies
Sube ...	... Sobanus ...	... Sabis
	Sapara ...	... [Asopus, Greece]
		Sinnus
Sinu	... Sonus	... Asinarus, Sicily
		[Sonus, Hibernia]

E

Other river names are—

America.	India and East.	West.
Caca, Bolivia ...	... Cacathis, I.	... Caicus, A. Minor
Cachy, Peru ...	... ——	Caicinus, Italy
		Cæcina, Italy
Chira, Peru ...	... ——	Akiris, Italy
Curaray, Peru	... ——	
Aguan, C. America	... Kainas, I.	...
Ulua, C. America	... ——	Ollius, Italy
Guapai, Bolivia	... Kophos, I.	... Gabellus, Italy
Montagua, C. America ...	——	Mitua, Macedonia
		Modoacus, Italy
Mira, Ecuader	... ——	Merula, Italy
Marona, Ecuader	... ——	Himera, Sicily
Mayo (river name), Peru,		
Mexico ...	... Mais, I. ...	...
Mantaro, Peru	... Manda, I	... Munda, Spain
Mapiri, Bolivia	... Mophis, I.	...
Lempa, C. America	... Lombare, I.	... Lambrus, Italy
Lacantum, C. America ...	——	Alukus, Italy
		Helicon, Italy
Nasas, Mexico	... ——	Anassus, Italy
Nape, Ecuader	... ——	Anapus, Sicily
		Enipeus, Macedonia
Pita, Ecuader...	... Catabeda, I. extra	... Padus, Italy
Piti, Mexico ...	... ——	Bœtis, Spain
Putu (mayo) Ecuader	... Spauto [lake]	... Pitanus, Corsica
Panuco, Mexico	... ——	[Benacus (lake), Italy, N.]
Bubo, Ecuader	... ——	Bæbe (lake), Greece
Babispe, Mexico	... ——	Fevos, Italy
Paso (mayo) Peru	... Hyphasis, India	... Pœsus, A. Minor
	Phasis, Colchis	...
Yapura, Ecuader	... ——	Hipparis, Italy
Rimac, Peru ...	... ——	Rubiko, Italy
Arispe, Mexico	... Zariaspis, Bactriano .	
Sirama, C. America	... Serus, India	... Siris, Italy
Ohosura, Mexico	... ——	Æsurus, Italy
Samala, C. America	... Sabalaessa, India ...	
Sintalapa, C. America	... Sandabalus, India	... Sontinus, Italy
Usumasinta, Mexico	... ——	Ossa, Italy
Sumbay, Peru	... Sambus, I.	...
Zacatula, Mexico	... ——	Sekies, Italy
		Tolenus, Italy
Tepitapa, C. America	... Attabas, I.	... Tobios, Britain
Tabasquillo, Mexico	... Tava, I. ..	... Tavis, Italy
Tambo, Peru ...	... ——	Timavus, Italy
Tula, Mexico ...	... ——	Tolenus, Italy
Dauli, Ecuader	... ——	Tilurus, Illyria
Tamoin, Mexico	... Temala, I. extra	... Tamion, Britain
Yavari, Peru ...	... Chaberis, India	...
Ica, Peru ...	... ——	Axios, Macedonia
Huasa, Peru ...	... ——	Æsis, Italy

With regard to lake names, they appear to be related to river names—

Lakes—America.		Old World (R) River.
Parras, Mexico	... ...	Prasias, Thessaly; Prasiane, India,W
Patzcuaro, Mexico	... ...	Gouraios (R), India
Chapala, Mexico	... ...	Copais, Bœotia

America—Lakes.		Old World (R) River.
Fuquene, Mexico	... ...	Fucinus, Italy, Sabine
Peten, Central America ...	...	Pitanus (R), Corsica
Amatitan, Central America	...	Andomatis (R), India
Tamiagua, Mexico	... ...	Tamion (R), Britain
Titicaca, Peru	... ...	Caicus (R), A. Minor; Cacathis (R), India
Chinchaycocha, Peru	... ...	Cainas (R), India

The identifications of Fuquene and Peten are striking.

In the reduction of mountain names very little fortune has ever attended me. The cause appears to be that few are Sumerian, that some are Agaw, and that some are most likely older.

America.		Old World.
Cotopaxi, Ecuador	... ...	Cottia, Alpes
Cotocha	... ...	Pactyas
Sangay, Ecuador	... ...	Syngaras, Mesopotamia
Tancitaro, Mexico	... ...	Cithæron, Greece
Orizava, Mexico	... ...	Oropeda, Spain
Apanecas, Central America	...	Pangæus, Macedonia
Assuay, Ecuader	... ...	Ossa, Greece
Pulla, Ecuader	... ...	Pelion, Greece
Ambato, Ecuader	... ...	Idubeda, Spain
		Bœtios, Drangiana
Atitlan, Central America	...,	Œta, Athos, Greece
		Ida, Asia Minor, etc.
Alausi, Ecuader	... ...	Alesion, Greece; Olgassys, A. Minor
Pasto, Ecuader	... ...	Phœstus, Greece
Perote, Mexico	... ...	Pierius, Greece
Merendon, Central America	...	Maro, Sicily
Cadlud, Ecuader	... ...	Cadmus

Some of these must be identical.

The town names are thus shown:—

Peru.	Mexico and Central America.	Old World.
*Arica... ...	—	*Arakha, Susiana
*Recuay ...	—	Arakhosia, Persia
Urcum ...	—	Arikaka, Arakhosia
,,	—.	Araxa, Lycia
,,	—	*Erech, Accad (Bible)
,,	—	*Rechah (Bible)
,,	—	Aricada, Drangiana
Arequipa ...	—	Aragorasa, Armenia
,,	—	Archabios, Colchis
,,	—	Arukanda, Lycia
,,	—	Argos, Greece
*Arapa ...	*Trapuata, Mexico ...	... *Arubath (Bible)
,,	Rabin, Central America	... Arabissus, Cappadocia
,,	—	Arbaka, Arakhosia
Yura ...	... Yoro, Central America	... Ora, India E.
Huaura ...	—	
*Oruro	... Aviare R, Central America	... *Oruras, A. Minor
,,	Arispe R, Central America	... Zariashes (R) Bactriana
Astobamba	... Iztapalapan, Mexico ...	... *Hasta, Liguria

Peru.	Mexico and Central America.	Old World.
*Huasta	—	Asta, Liguria and Lusitania
,,	—	Ashdod (Bible)
,,	—	Astasanna, Aria
,,	—	Asthagura, India E.
,,	—	Astakapra ,,
Ambato, M	... Ambalema, New Granada	...
*Acoramba	... —	*Corombo (R) Carmania
Illampe, M	... —	Cosamba, India S.
Cosapa	... *Cosuma, Yucatan	... *Cosamba, India S.
Casma	... —	
Cuzmo	... —	
*Chosica	... *Cuisco, Mexico ...	... *Cuzikos, A. Minor
*Cuzco	... Chuscal, New Granada	... *Gauzaka, Paropamisada
Quisco	... —	Choastra, Media
Congata	... Concanu, Yucatan ...	... Concana, Spain
Canchari	... Conagua, New Granada	... Iconium, A. Minor
Chancay	... Conchagua, Central America .	Xoana, India
Conongo	... —	Gain, Palestine
Acañ ...	... —	Aquinium, Italy
Quinoa	... —	
*Cacary	... Cacahuamilpa, Mexico	... *Acharacha, Caria
Caquiaviria	... Chiquisa, New Granada	... Gaggra, Paphlagonia
,,	—	Gagasmira, India E.
Chiclayo	... Cochilha, New Granada	... Cocala, India S.
*Chepen	... *Copan, Central America	... *Cabena, Media
,,	*Coban, Guatemala ...	... *Capena, Etruria
,,	—	*Cabbon, Palestine
,,	—	Cepiana, Lusitania
,,	Caparrapi, New Granada	... Caberasa, Media
,,	*Chipata, New Granada	... Caption, Sicily
,,	—	*Gibbeath, Palestine
*Chipaya	... *Kabah, Yucatan ...	... Cuba, India S.
,,	Chepo, New Granada ...	... *Capua, Italy
,,	—	*Gaba, Palestine
,,	—	Gabii, Italy
,,	*Chapala, Mexico	... *Capula, Venetia
,,	*Chapul, Mexico	... Cubilia, Lycia
,,	Acapulco, Mexico	...
,,	—	*Cabale, Media
,,	—	Cabul, Palestine
Talcanta	... Cundinamarca, New Granada.	Conta, India E.
,,		Aricanda, A. Minor
Quillo ...	... *Akil, Yucatan	... *Aquileia, Italy
,,	Chollolan, Mexico	...
,,	—	Kaloe, Lydia
,,	—	Keilah, Palestine
,,	—	Agylla, Etruria
,,	—	Akela, Media
Chilca ...	... ——	*Chalcis, Bœotia
Quellca	... *Chalco, Mexico ...	... Gilgal, Palestine
Colca ...	... Chalcicomula, Mexico ...	...
,,	*Colosa, New Granada	... *Colossai, Phrygia
,,	Chalisco, Mexico ...	... Akalissos, Pontus
*Chumu	... Comayagua, Honduras	... *Cume, Mysia
*Caime	... *Cuame, New Granada	... *Cumæ, Italy
,,	Chima, New Granada	... Choma, Pisidia
*Cambe	... —	*Cambe, Gedrosia
Combapata	...	
Chicamo	... *Cucumba, New Granada	... *Cocambo, Gedrosia
*Camana	... —	*Comania, Caria

Peru.	Mexico and Central America.	Old World.
*Guamani	... *Guaman, Mexico ...	... *Comana, Pontus and Capp.
,,	—	Cominium, Samnium
,,	Guaymas ...	... Chemosh (Bible)
,,	—	Gimza (Bible)
,,	—	Camisa, Cappadocia
*Chimeroo ...	—	*Kimara, India E.
*Catari	... *Chatura, New Granada	... *Cytorus, Armenia
,,	*Cadereita, Mexico ...	... *Coddura, India S.
,,	Catarumbo R, New Granada...	Cottiara, India S.
,,	—	Cotuora, Pontus
Quito ...	... *Cuaita, New Granada	... Kattah, Palestine
*Coati...	... Oicata, New Granada...	... *Cuta, Colchis
,,	—	*Caudium, Sabine
*Chatuna ...	—	*Catana, Sicily
*Costaparaca .	—	*Cotobara, India S.
Costabamba ...	—	*Cottobara, Gedrosia
Curaray, R ...	*Carere R, New Granada	... *Careura, Caria and India
*Ocaruro ...		
,,	Charala, New Granada	... Curula, India S.
*Charasani ...	—	*Caresena, Mysia
Charcani	... Chiriguana, New Granada	... Corcobana, Ceylon
*Chuana	... Chanaco, Mexico ...	... Kanah, Palestine
,,	Canipauna, New Granada	... Kana, Mysia
,,	Cunacua, New Granada	... Kœne, Cappadocia
,,	—	*Canagara, India S.
*Caracona ...	—	*Aganagara, India extra.
,,		Khoana, Parthia
Ocona...	... Ocansip, Yucatan	... Aganagara, India extra.
*Ascona ...	—	*Oskana, Gedrosia
,,	—	*Assecona, Spain
*Acora ...	—	*Acarra, Susiana
*Acari ...	—	*Achor, Palestine
Acoramba ...	—	*Cora, Lalutus
Corocuero ...	—	Agiria, Spain
*Ancon ...	—	*Ancona, Italy
Hancane ...	—	
*Colan	... Calan, Yucatan	... Calneh, Accar (Bible)
,,	—	*Gelan, Palestine
Calanacoche ...	—	Calindoca, India S.
*Calasnique ...	—	Calinaxa, India S.
,,	*Oculan, Mexico	... Okelum, Lusitania
,,	—	Akelanum, Sabine
Cailloma	... Caluma, Ecuador ...	... Gallim, Palestine
Calupe	... Jalapa, Mexico and C. Amer. .	Calpe, M.
Challapa	... Jutigalpac, America	... Haran (Bible)
Ocharan ...	—	
,,	*Garupa, New Granada	... Acharna, Attica
Caropango ...	*Labna, Yucatan...	... *Gariphus, India
Llapo ...	... *Labhakhabpha, Yucatan	... *Labbana, Mesopotamia
,, ...	—	*Labaca, India S.
Lambayeque...	Lampa, Salvador ...	... Alambatesa, Comaria
Illampo, M ...	Liborina, New Granada	... Lampsacus, A. Minor
,,	—	Lombare, India
Larecaja ...	—	Lariaga, India E.
Mantaro ...	Huamantla, Mexico	... Mendola, India S.
*Manani ...	Mani, Yucatan ...	... *Maniæna, India E.
Mani	—	Amana, Media
Mirinavis ...	Merindon, Honduras	... Morunda, Media
Marona ...	—	
Machurana ...	Macaranita, New Granada	... Magaris, India S.

Peru.	Mexico and Central America.	Old World.
Machurana	... Mogorontoque, New Granada	Mogarus, Pontus
„	—	Makrasa, Lycia
•Macari	... —	*Megara, Gr., Sicily
„	Mozca, Mexico ...	... Maxere, Hyrcania
„	Mescala „ ...	„
„	•Mogote, New Granada	... Maguda, Mesopotamia
•Malla	... —	*Mala, Pontus
„	—	Millo, Palestine
Amiloe	... —	Amilos, Arcadia
Mantaro	... —	Manda, India
*Marcara	... —	*Margara, India E.
•Marcomarcani	Cundinamarca ...	... *Margana, Ceylon
„	—	Maricada, Bactriana
„	•Margua (R) New Granada	... *Margus (R) Margiane
„	•Masaya, Yucatan	... *Massah, Palestine
„	—	*Amasia, Pontus
•Masin	... —	*Messana, Sicily
„	—	Messene, Greece
•Mapiri, R	... —	*Mapura (R), India
•Napo...	... *Neyba, New Granada	... *Nebo (Bible)
„	—	Nebah (Bible)
„	—	*Nepea, Phrygia
•Nasca	... —	*Nasica, India S.
Nanasca	... *Nunkini, Yucatan	... *Nanaguna, India S.
„	Nicaragua, C. America	... Nuceria (?), Italy
„	—	Anaguros, Greece
„	Nimaima, New Granada	... Nommana, Carmania
„	Nare „	... Nar, Italy
„	—	Anara, India S.
•Unanue	... —	*Ninue, Nineveh
„	—	(Accad) Bible
„	Oiba, New Granada	... Ophia, Sabine
„	Upia „	... Aphia, Phrygia
(Pucara, castle)	—	[cara, castle, Akkad]
•Pucara	... •Bucaramanga, New Granada	*Begorra, Macedonia
•Pucala	... —	*Pygela, Ionia
„	—	Pegella, Lycaonia
Azangari	... —	Agara, Susiana
„	—	„ India S.
Patapa	... [Patawi, Siam] ...	... Patavium, Bythinia
Patavilca	... —	„ Italy
Pataz ...	... —	
*Paita...	... Pauta, New Granada	... *Bata, India S.
Ayapata	... •Pitu, Mexico ...	... Beda, Mesopotamia
*Pita ...	... Peto, Yucatan ...	... *Pida, Pontus
Putu ...	... *Ubate, New Granada	... *Eboda, Palestine
„	—	Pitueia, Mysia
„	—	Phauda, Pontus
*Putina	... *Peten, Yucatan ...	... *Pitane, Mysia
„	Potonchan, Yucatan	... *Padua, Palestine
„	—	Bitoana, Caria
Piura ...	... Perote, Mexico ...	... Pieria, Greece
Yapura	... —	„ Syria
„	—	Phiarasa, Pontus
•Pitura	... *Paturia, New Granada	... *Patara, Lycia
„	Necopetara, Mexico	... Badara, Carnithia
„	—	Sobatra, Lycaonia
„	*Zupetara, C. America	... *Opetura, India
„	Sopetran, New Granada	...
*Paria	... *Para „	... *Parium

Peru.	Mexico and Central America.	Old World.
Paria ...	... Paracheque, New Granada	... Pyrrha, Caria
,,	Ibarra, Ecuader ...	... Birei, Palestine
Parara ...	—	Podoperura, India extra.
Pararin ...		
,,	Parras, Mexico ...	... Parisara ,,
,,	*Barichara, New Granada	... *Barakura ,,
*Parac ...	... Parachoque ,,	... *Berachah, Palestine
Cotaparaco ...	—	Pharugia, Doris
Pariache ...	—	Verrugo, Latium
Pariacote ...	—	Barkine, Spain
Paruchay ...	—	
Puno	—	*Punon, Palestine
*Punyon ...	—	Panion, Thessaly
Panos	—	
Pando	—	Pandassa, India extra
*Papai ...	... *Paipa, New Granada	... *Papha, Pisidia
Babo	—	*Paphos, Cyprus
*Pusi	—	*Pisæ (3)
Puzuzi ...	—	*Paseah, Palestine
*Pasa (mayo) ...	—	*Ephesus, A. Minor
Pisagua ...	—	*Phoizoi, Arcadia
(Pirca Quichua Wall, Enclosure) ...	—	Pergamos
,,	—	Perga, Pamphylia
,,	—	Pyrgih, Etruria
*Pomalca ...	... *Paime, New Granada	... *Bamala, India S.
		*Apamea, Parthia
Pichigua ...	... Bogota ,,	... Phecis, Greece
Puquien ...	... Pachuco, Mexico ...	... Phokaia, Lydia
Pacas (mayo) ...	—	Pauka, Italy
Palalayuca ...		Palalke, Pontus
,,	Bolonchan, Yucatan	... Bolon, Spain
,,	—	Pelon, Palestine
*Pasco ...	... Tobasco, Yucatan	... *Boskath, Palestine
*Posco ...	—	Bezek, Palestine
*Pisco ...	—	*Phuska, Macedonia
Piscahacha ...	—	*Physkus, Caria
Pacsi	—	Paxos I.
*Pista ...	... *Piste, Yucatan ...	... *Pœstum, Italy
Arambolu ...	... *Arama, New Granada	... *Aruma (Bible)
,,	—	*Aroma, Caria
,,	—	Ariminium, Italy
*Racanya ...	... *Ariguani, New Granada	... *Rakkon (Bible)
Tacaraca ...	—	*Oricana, Media
,,	—	Arucanda, Lycia
,,	Raquira, New Granada	... Aragorasa, Armenia
,,	Sinu ,,	... Sena, Etruria and Umbria
,,	—	Zaananim (Bible)
,,	Sanalarga ,,	... Sannala, India E.
,,	*Sinoloa, Mexico ...	...
,,	Sonora ,, ...	... Posinara, India E.
,,	—	Asinarus, Sicily
Aposungo ...	... Okosingo, Yucatan	... Sangada, India E.
Sangay ...	... Texancingo, Mexico	... Sangala, ,,
*Charasani ...	—	Alosanga, India extra.
,,	—	Caresena, Mysia
Antisana ...	—	Astasanna, Aria
*Sanagoran ...	—	*Suanagora, India extra.
,,	*Sonsonate, S. Salvador	... *Sansannah (Bible)

Peru.	Mexico and Central America.	Old World.
*Sanagoran ...	*Tzintzontzon, Mexico	... *Susonnia, Venetia
,,	—	*Nazianxene, Cappadocia
,,	*Sonson, New Granada	... *Saniseni, Paphlagonia
,,	Site ,,	... Side, Pamphyl., Laconia
,,	Suta ,,	... Sidas, Greece
,,	*Susa ,,	... *Suzah, Palestine
,,	—	Susa, Susiana
,,	Susagua ,,	... Suissa, Cappadocia
,,	—	Suessa (R), Italy
,,	—	Suassus, India
,,	*Susacon, New Granada	... *Susicana, India E.
Soroche	—	Syracuse, Sicily
Surco ...	—	Saraka, Media
,,	—	Sariga, Armenia
,,	—	Saruge, A. Minor
Sorata	... Surata, New Granada	... Sarid, Palestine
,,	*Sarare, New Granada	... *Sararra, Mesopotamia
*Sikuani	*Sura ,,	... *Saura, Susiana
*Sikuani	—	Saganus, Carmania
,,	—	*Saguana, Armenia
,,	—	*Sakovna, Belicia
,,	—	*Sikuon, Greece
*Succha	...	*Saca, Arcadia
Sachaca	... Sachica, New Granada	...
Sacayacu	... Soacha ,,	...
,,	Sacota ,,	... Adisaga, Media
Sikasika	... Segamoso ,,	... Sakasena, Cappadocia
,,	Fusugasuga ,,	... Zazaka, Media
,,	Zaccacal, Yucatan	... Secacah, Palestine
Sogon ...	...	— Sikinos, I.
Sechura	...	— Shicron (Bible)
,,	*Salli, Yucatan ...	... *Sala, Armenia
,,	*Zelaya, Mexico ...	... *Sela, Palestine
Sullillica	... Zulia, New Granada	... *Solia, Spain
,,	*Salamo, Guatemala	... *Salamis, (?)
,,	Salmaguela, New Granada	... *Zalmoneh, Palestine
,,	—	Salmantike,
Suyana	... *Senote, Yucatan	... Aznoth, Palestine
,,	—	*Sunnada, Phrygia
,,	Zerna, New Granada	... Sarnuka, Mesopotamia
,,	*Zema ,,	... *Shema (Bible)
,,	Zimapan, Mexico...	... Ezem ,,
,,	—	*Zama, Capp. and Mesopo.
Saman	... Semindoco, New Granada	... Semina, Parthia
,,	*Samala, C. America	... *Simyla, India S.
*Sumbay, R ...	—	*Sambus (R), India
*Supe ...	... *Saboya, New Granada	... Sabius, Cappadocia
Monsifu	... *Sube, Sura ,,	... Zaba, India extra
,,	—	*Zobia, Pisidia
,,	—	Shebah (Bible)
,,	Yzabal, C. America	... Sapolus, India extra
*Zepita	...	— *Zephath, Palestine
Zapatoca	...	— Sibecla, Lycia
,,	*Zupetara, New Granada	... *Sabatra, Lycaonia
,,	Sopetran ,,	...
*Atocama	...	— *Attacum, Spain
Tucuma	... Tocaima ,,	...
*Tauca	... *Togui ,,	... *Tugea, Spain
,,	—	*Tukki, Spain
,,	—	Athach (Bible)

Peru.	Mexico and Central America.	Old World.
*Tauca	—	*Techoa, Palestine
,,	*Tekoh, Yucatan...	... Tegea, Greece
,,	Tacubaya, Mexico	... *Thagora, India extra.
Tacaraca	... *Tachira, New Granada	... *Tagara, India S.
Tuquilipon	... Tacaloa ,,	... Taxila, India E.
,,	Tekit	... Attagus, Bœotia
Tarapaca	...	Tarrago, Spain
,,	*Tolima, New Granada	... *Telem (Bible)
,,	*Toloman, Guatemala	... *Telamo
,,	Tuloom, Yucatan	... *Telamina, Spain
*Thalambo	... —	*Teleboas, A. Minor
,,	Tulapan ...	... Tholobona, India S.
Dauli ...	... Tolla, Mexico ...	...
,,	Tolo, New Granada	...
,,	Tula, Mexico ...	...
,,	Tollan, Mexico ...	... Dolion, Bœotia
,,	Delen, New Granada	... Dolionis, Mysia
,,	—	Tullonium, Spain
,,	—	Dilean, Palestine
Tarma	—	Atarmes, Bactriana
,,	—	Tarbakana, Paropanisada
,,	*Tabi, Yucatan ...	... *Taba, Phrygia, Caria
,,	Teabo, Yucatan ...	... Thebæ, Bœotia, Thessaly
Tabatingo	... Tabeo, New Granada	... Tebbath, Palestine
Tapacoche	... Tabachula, Guatemala	... Tapuah, Palestine
,,	Tabasquillo, Mexico	... Thebez, Palestine
*Tipuani	... Tepan, Mexico ...	... *Tabiene, A. Minor
,,	*Tibaria, New Grenada	... *Thebura, Assyria
,,	Tubar, Mexico ...	...
,,	*Tapata, New Granada	... *Tobata, Paphlagonia
,,	Topia, Mexico ...	...
,,	Tobasco, Yucatan	... Thapsacus, Syria
Tuman	... Tamoin, Mexico ...	... Dimonah (Bible)
,,	—	Temani ,,
Tumbo	... *Tampico, Mexico	... Tumnos, Caria
Tambo	... Temisco ,, ...	... *Tamassis, India E.
,,	*Tamasinchali, Mexico ...	
,,	*Tamalameque, New Granada	*Temala, India extra.
,,	Tumila ,,	
,,	*Tamar ,,	*Tamarus, India
,,	Tanquichi, Mexico	... Taanach (Bible)
,,	Tenochtitlan ,,	...
,,	*Tena, New Granada	... *Toana, India extra
,,	Tizimin, Yucatan	... Tisia, Italy
,,	Tiza[pan], Mexico	... Tisa, Carmania
,,	Tausa, New Granada	... Tiausa, India
,,	Tuz[pan] ...	... Dosa, Assyria

The Accad cities mentioned in the Bible, in Genesis x, v. 10, 11, 12, besides Babel, Accad, and Rehoboth, are :—

Erech	compare ...	... Arica, Peru
Calneh	,, ...	... Calanoche (Peru), Oculan
Ninue or Nineveh	,, ...	... Unanue, Peru
Calah	,, ...	... Colacote ,,
Resen	,, ...	... Charasani ,,

Many cities in Palestine are closely represented.

A circumstance worthy of remark, and which may indicate

Sumerian influence in Brazil, if not that the Sumerians had settlements there, is that the Guarani word for town is Taba, that is Taba, Thebes, etc., of geography, the Daba of the present Georgians. If the Sumerians had at any time a settlement on the great river mouths, the passage of the Atlantic would be credible, and the knowledge of the Atlantic ocean by the geographers of Babylonia and Pergamos accounted for.

Under this head of topographical nomenclature, a course of investigation is being pursued by the Rev. Professor John Campbell of Montreal, and formerly of Toronto, which can be consulted with great advantage.

In the "Canadian Journal," and under the titles of the "Horites" and of "The Shepherd Kings of Egypt," Prof. Campbell has adopted as his basis the genealogies of the books of Genesis, Kings, and Chronicles. With the help of the Egyptian and classic data, he is bringing to bear a flood of light upon the Sumerian epoch of civilisation with regard to the genesis and migration of nations, and the mythology of the period. All tends to illustrate the importance of the protohistoric era.

Much of this work is necessarily tentative, and although there are few illustrations with regard to America, these memoirs can be profitably consulted by the investigator in common with those of Lenormant and the Egyptologists. Of course in Bryant and many of the old mythologists many of the collateral facts may be found, but treated in a manner incompatible with our present knowledge.

Upon the grand question of the population of Canaan, Professor Campbell gives us invaluable materials for forming a judgment. This population most probably extended into Egypt, where Brugsch Bey has found 400 parallel names, and in which I look for the "Turanian" element. Thebes, and the other old names by which Egypt was known to the Greeks are Sumerian. The intercourse with Caria long continued. The union of Sumerians with Semites explains the ethnological peculiarities of the Jews, who are evidently a mixed race with two elements.

As to the ancient extent of the Sumerian region in America, it cannot yet be determined, for it must have been wider than at the Spanish Conquest, but with regard to the names here given for the New World and the Old, it must be borne in mind that some are Agaw, and extend into Brazil. The consideration of the Brazilian river names gives us a test in relation to those of Europe, and they confirm the opinion I have given of an Agaw influence in Europe anterior to the Sumerian, and which will have to be taken into account by the craniologist. He has to provide for the Vasco-Kolarian, the Agaw, and the Sumerian migrations.

The whole of the phenomena of man in America represent an arrested development of civilisation, cut short as compared with Europe and Asia, not by climate, as in Africa, and yet quite sufficient to include the two epochs of great stone monuments and of palatial works with inscriptions, epochs which embraced the first spiritualised religion, that of the worship of light; a time of thousands of years, so remote that, in the old world, it has now only its scanty votaries among the Parsees of Bombay. Time, too, so remote, that the great religions of the globe, Judaism, Christianity, and Islam had, with Buddhism, got time to expand and to cover the eastern hemisphere, while, until the Spanish conquest, the Americas had, in the flux of centuries, never heard their revelations.   Few things so strongly pourtray the deep, dark gulf of separation as this, when associations which had been commonly shared from the beginning of mankind, were snapped in the time of their deepest interest and moment, and it was hazard, and not design, placed the Indians that perished and the Indians that continued under the teaching of the missionaries of Spain and Portugal, and which all have not yet known.

The evidence of language comes in support of this arrest of development, for there are no languages in America of the later and higher forms.   When the early Akkad stopped, there all stop.   This it is which gives the false impression of there being a peculiar and special American grammar.   This has been so specially studied and treated, whereas, the languages in America, which cannot be rightly called American languages, are under the same conditions of prehistoric grammar as the earlier languages of the old world.   The grammar of Omagua may be as truly called Caucasian as American, and, if we choose, that of Abkhas might be as rightly named American as Caucasian.

As there was in the furthest or prehistoric days a stream of emigration continuously from the old world to the new, the question arises whether this set back again, and whether a knowledge of the new world was carried to the old.   The first set of population appears to have been over Behring's Straits, or across the narrow seas, and migrations which could cover the eastern world, even with Akkas and Bushmen from Lapland to South Africa, would be able to fill America from the snowy pole to Tierra del Fuego, as there is witness enough to show, in blood, in speech, and in folk-lore.

It is very questionable whether at any time there was regular intercourse over the Atlantic, for that would have needed ships, and a trade once set up, other animals besides dogs, and other plants than those now found, would have followed man.

In what we know of the historical period, under the Greeks

and the Romans, a lively knowledge of America was lost; the Greeks could not reach it from the west, and the Romans, when they settled on the shores of the Atlantic, had other cares than to risk the wide, dark sea.

A dead knowledge lingered, not only of the geography of the Americas, but of Australasia, which is of no less interest with regard to the latter region, because that exhibits, philologically, evidence of early migrations of the Mincopie or Pygmean in Borneo, of the Sandeh or Niam-Niam of the Nile in Tasmania, and of the Agaw in Galela, and in the other languages recorded by Wallace.

There was indeed a system of geography long prevalent among the ancients and in the dark ages, which is referred to in the Timæus of Plato, and was notably maintained by Crates of Pergamos, 160 B.C. (Reinaud, " Journal Asiatique", vol. i, new series, 1863, p. 140), and also referred to by Virgil in the Æneid. Four inhabited worlds were treated of, and there appears to have been, in traditions, an imperial title of Monarch of the Four Worlds. This I connect with the statement of Mr. George Smith that Agu, an ancient king of Babylonia, called himself King of the Four Races. Again, with Prescott, who, in the " Conquest of Peru," book i, ch. ii, says,—" It is certain that the natives had no other epithet by which to designate the large collection of tribes and nations who were assembled under the empire of the Incas, than that of Tavintinsuyu or Four Quarters of the World." He quotes Ondegarde, Rel. Prim. MSS, and Garcilasso, Comentarie Real, ii, 11. This title was perhaps a prerogative of the middle king, or monarch of the middle kingdom, of the great civilized empire of the world. The Chinese preserve the tradition of the middle kingdom, the trinary having followed the quarternary system. Thus, in Genesis there are three sons of Noah. The Vedas refer to three worlds.

The nomenclature of Ptolemy and the other geographers is of the Akkad epoch, and that of the early Biblical books, Akkad or Babylonian.

The school of Pergamos taught that the world, which must have been treated as a sphere, contained four worlds. Ours was one of these, and as is true in Asia that it does not cross the line, so it was supposed that Africa does not cross the line, and the Babylonian geographers were well acquainted with Southern Asia but not with Southern Africa. This Northern World was balanced by an Austral World, and this is so, depicting the Australasian Islands, the scene of Sumerian migrations, and Australia, which was known to them. Australia was, by the Sumerians as by far later geographers, supposed to extend from opposite Asia, as a Terra Incognita of the maps, opposite Africa.

A not less remarkable affirmation was, that the Northern World and that of Australia were balanced on the other side of the globe also by a Northern World and continent and by a Southern World, and this is so in North and South America.

It was said, being nigh the truth, that these four worlds were cut off by belts of ocean, one from north to south, and by another running round the middle of the world from east to west. Such ocean we know shuts off Asia from Australia, and those ancients might be forgiven, who drew a sea over the narrow necks between North and South America, which must then as now have been passed by canoes at passages on the Atrato and on other rivers.

These four worlds were alleged to have their men, as we know they had and have, but to account amid so much truth for intercourse not taking place between them in their days, a fable was got up that the seas were made impassable. The philosophers, however, forgot to tell us how the knowledge of these other worlds and the men in them was gained. Gained too, it was, and lost by the cessation of intercourse, after the Sumerians, with the Americas. This was perhaps owing to the rise of a great power in China, which disturbed the road from India, and the seats of kingdom in Southern Asia.

How that dream of a true globe and its continents and people reached the Greeks and Romans, and how it suggested to the flatterers of Augustus a title of monarch of those four worlds, is here accounted for. It must be traced beyond Pergamos to those older schools of learning, known to us under such a name as Chaldean, but which had flourished in protohistoric epochs from the dawn of civilisation.

There must at one time have been in the olden world, men who could bring back this knowledge of the Americas from their Nineveh to its Nineveh and Babel, where the empire of the four worlds got centred, and where one language was spoken and written for the government of the earth. How truly was it then said of Babel, "And the whole earth was of one language, and of one speech" (Genesis xi, 1).

The fall of that power was indeed confusion of nations and of tongues.

After a time, the tradition alone of these other worlds lingered, as we have seen, as a theory of cosmography ; lingering to be condemned by the Christian church, as a thing that men of learning ought not to learn, but reproduced in our own language by Sir John Mandeville. He insisted that the world was a globe and could be circumnavigated, and he tells a tale of a man from Norway, who had gone so long by land and by sea that he had environed all the earth, that he was come about to his own marches.

The intercourse in times of yore between the new world and the old, now again brought to light, rests upon no slight evidence, although the whole of it cannot be included here. It comes in confirmation of the labours of those who have gone before me, and of my own, carried on step by step for some time.*

The relationship of the topographical nomenclature and of the languages of the old world with those of the new, was laid down by me in my paper, on the "Comparative Grammar of the Egyptians," last year. What is now published, is the development and detail of the same principles which had occupied me for many years, but which have not till now been brought nearer to complete exemplification.

It may be briefly said that my object now has been to show the development of language in prehistoric grammar, and the unity of language in all continents, and more particularly the unity of culture generally throughout the world, by dealing with what has been regarded as the exceptional position of America. Many points are not touched, not from want of knowledge, but want of space. All that has been here stated will be found in conformity with the results obtained by other inquirers on the prehistoric and protohistoric epochs, and will throw a light upon their labours. It is hoped that many portions will, in this respect, be found of general use beyond their special application.

The development of language, mythology, and culture generally, the migrations of nations, the naming of animals, the naming of mountains, of rivers, and of towns, are here illustrated, not only in the infancy of mankind, but in the institution of a great civilisation, so ancient that its traditions had become dim, and that its history has to be recovered from beneath the rubbish mounds of its cities.

The history of the fall of such empires, and of such kingdoms, is a tempting subject, but it is one which belongs rather to the historian, for it took place in the ages of history, than to the students of the Anthropological Institute. The results may, however, be considered by us, for they show that the history of savagedom and of civilisation is the same for both halves of the globe. In America the forms of savagedom are better preserved and these give us some of the most valuable elements for filling up what is on our side wanting.

The American materials are also of none the less value because

* See various papers of mine in the Journals of the Ethnological Society, of the Anthropological Institute, of the Palestine Exploration Fund, etc.

they help to build up the uniform history of civilisation, of progress, which may be long delayed by barbarism, but cannot in the end be checked. It is a progress amid which, while the oldest and rudest races may still live, their rudest propensities and habits are doomed to decay, and their bloodiest superstitions to be abandoned.

The philological considerations are, in this sense, also of interest, because language is not only as here used a history of culture, but a great and living instrument of culture. Its influence is, of course, a disturbing one as well, and hence, although not decisive for ethnological determination, it is none the less to be regarded. Speech is the heir, the representative, the transmitter of the accumulated experience of civilisation in thousands of years. Hence its apostolic power. In proportion to the improved capacity of transmission in cultivated languages, so will such languages influence a lower race to which they are communicated, and by which they are used. So a low race acquiring a high language becomes more capable of improvement, and makes greater advances than the low race which retains a rude tongue.

Of this there are examples enough, and in Central and South America the acquirement of the Spanish tongue has given large populations means of advancement which they do not possess in the Quichua or Maya, which were before written, any more than in Guarani, which the Jesuits put in writing. By the help of Spanish the people and their leaders of pure Indian blood now in power, have become orators, poets, lawyers, able to take place alongside of those of old Spain. The effect of race remains, but a great advance is due to speech.

The fusion of race wished for by some can only be effected by the deterioration of the better, or it will be compensated for by the practical annihilation of the weaker; but the fusion of language is a great and safe instrument for bringing about among various populations a harmony of civilisation. English will thus act in India. It is civilisation which is the best heritage of mankind, and the more this can be brought within the compass of all, even of the meanest, the greater will be the benefit conferred upon the whole.

Appendix Table of Sumerian Words.

The following is a brief list of words divided [into three regions, the American including two columns, and while in some cases a root may be traced throughout, it will be seen that more commonly the western and American roots or types cross in the Indo-Chinese region. This table may be much extended.

Ak., Akkad.   *Cam.*, Cambodian *Aym.*, Aymara.   *Mex.*, Aztek.
C., Circassian.   *Mon*, Peguan.   *Q.*, Quichua.   *Oth.*, Othomi.
G., Georgian.   *Bu.*, Burmese.   *Tava.*, Tarahum-
           Ann., Annam.   ara.
                                                Huas., Huasteca
                                                Poc., Poconchi.

	Western.	Indo-Chinese.	Peruvian.	Mexican, etc.
Man	... karra, Ak.	... karu, Mon	... kkari, Aym., Q.	.. [ucari, Cora]
	mulu, Ak.	... lu, Burmese	—	
	kmari, Geo.	... [mairima, Bu., woman]	—	
	tle, Circas.	...	—	tlacatl. Huas.
	gun, un, Ak.	... hplun, Mon	... runa, Q.	... uinic, Mex.
		khon, Siam ...	—	ninic, Maya
		kon, Shan ...	—	[akun, Poc.; boy]
	ku, Akkad	... paka, Mon	... chacha, Aym.	... nxihi, Oth.
		nguoi, Annam	... kosa, Q.	... oquich, Mex.
Woman, etc.	... sak, Akkad	... [su, man, Bu.]	.. [kosa, Q., man]	. nsu, Othomi
	shooz, Circ.	... —	—	soua, Mexico
	rak (a) Ak.	... —	rakka, Q.	...
	mak, Akkad	... meingma, Bu.]	.. marmi, Aym.	... muki, Tara.
		mairima, Bu. ...	—	
	dam, Akkad	... phdey, Cam. ...	—	[dame, Oth.]
				[tomol, Huas.]
Head	... ku, Akkad	... kbal, Camb.	... ppekei, Aym. ...	
	su, Akkad	... katau, Mon ...	—	
	shha, Circ.	... ko, Karen ...	—	ayxacaTotonaca
		kamon, Annam. uma, Q.	... hool, Mex.	
		alu, Kumi ...		moola, Tara.
Hair	... sik, Akkad	... sac, Cambo.	... suncca, Aym.	... xta, si, Oth.
	shhatsey, Cir.	... swet, Ann.	... socco, Q.	... tzotz, Mex.
		asham, Kumi ...		
Face	... ka, Akkad	—	akanu, Aym.	... axaya, Mex.
	piri, Georg.	... —	riccay, Q.	... [Maya
Eye	... limta, Ak.	... ta, Annam	... [mata, forehead, tahnaluich,	
	twali, Georg.	... panek, Cam. ...	—	Q. ghual, Maya
	nee, Circ.	... mitthah, An.	... naira, Aym.	... nich, Mex.
	si, Akkad	... —	nagui, Q.	... pusiki, Tara.
Ear	... pi, Akkad	... pik, Ahom ...	—	
	tal, Akkad	... khato, Mon ..	—	gu, Othomi
	quri, Georg.	... nakhu, Karen	... rincri, Q.	... nacaz, Mex.
	takumah, Circ.	... tai, Annam	... hinchu, Aym.	... necbkala, Tara.
Mouth	... ka, gu, Ak.	... amaka, Kami	... lakka, Aym.	... kama, Huas.
	dzheh, shey, C.	kha, Mon	... simi, Q.	... chi, Mex., Poc.
Tooth	... dzeh, Circas.	... zhua, Mon	... kchaka, Aym.	... tzi, Oth.
Forehead	tik, Akkad	... —	mati, Q.	...
	thkhemi, Geo. ...	—		
Tongue	... eme, Akkad	... —		qbane, Oth.
	ena, Georg.	... —		tenilla, Tara.
				zimagat, Toto
Heart	... sa, Akkad	... zeit, Bu.	... soncco, Q.	...
	libis, Akkad	... lao, Annam	... chuimo, Aym.	...
	guli, Georg.	... chai, Siam ...	—	
	ghey, Circ.	...	—	
Blood	... us, Akkad	... htseihn, Mon	... qhi, Oth.	...
	sishkhli, Georg.	swe, Bur.	... estli, Huast	...
			xihtz, Maya.	...
Hand	... sugab, Ak.	... su, Karen	... maqui, Q.	... cab, Mex.
	kheli, Georg.	... ka, Kumi, Ahom tachlli, Aym.	... cubac, Maya	

	Western.	Indo-Chinese.	Peruvian.	Mexican, etc.
Hand	... ia, oyg, Circ.	... mo, Annam ...	—	maco, Totonaca
Foot	... arik(i), Ak.	... kaw, Karen	... kayu, Aym.	... gua, Oth.
	pekhi, perhi, G.	shon, Siam	... chaqui, Q.	.. acan, Maya
	tlake, Circ.	...akho, Kami	—	tala, Tara.
Horn	... shi, Akkad	...sung, Annam	... huakra, Aym., Q.	
	rka, Georg.	... khyo, Bur. ...	—	
Skin	... shu, Akkad	...sare, axa, Bu....	ccara, Q. ...	
	kani, Georg. ...	—	lepitchi, Aym....	
	shooway, Circ....	—		
Sun	... zal(a), Akkad ...	—	inti, Aym., Q. ...	bindi, Oth.
	[usil Etrus] ...	—	—	tonatuih, Mex.
	mze, Georg. ...	—	lupi, Aym. ...	
	pushur, par, Ak.	—	punchau, Q. ...	
	teigha, Circ. ...	—	—	taika, Tarah.
	dgeh, Circas. ...	—	—	quih, Poc.
				aquicha, Huas.
Moon	... lid, Akkad	...la,Bur., lah,Kar.	quilla, Q.	... citlali, Mex. *w n up*
	[lala, Etr.]	...hpyalit, Siam...	—	
	es, Akkad ...	—	paksi, Aym.	... maitsaka, Tara.
	maathe, Circ. ...	—	—	
Star	...ooshaghe, Circ..	tsah, Karen	... sillo, Aym.	... tze, Othomi
	—	—		citlali, Mex.
Day	... dghe, Georg.	...thngay, Cam. ...		aquicha, Huas.
	[ur, Ak., light]	..ngay, Ann.	...uru, Aym.	...quib, Poc.
	tam, Akkad	... tangway, Mon .	—	[tonatuih, Mex.,
Fire	... ne, Akkad	...[ne,na,Bur.sun]	nina, Q., Aym..	[sun]
	kum, Akkad	...kamo, Camb. ...	—	naiki, Tara.
	[nefney, Cir.,			
	light]	—	—	
Water	... a, Akkad	...ya, Bur.	... yaku, Q., Aym..	ahti, Cora
	—	o, Sak. ...	—	a, Mex.; ye, Tar.
	aan, Ak[rain]	... nan, Siam	... unu, Q.	... ha, Maya
River	... aria, Akkad	...[re, Bur., water]	hahuiri, Aym....	
	mdinare, Geo....	mrach, Burm....	—	
	ada, Akkad	...tak, Camb. ...		atoya,Mex., Cor.
	ra, Ak., flow ...	—	—	
Sky, Heaven	... siku, sigaru, Ak.	kor, Camb. ...		kaan, Maya
	an, Akkad	...kani, Kumi ...	—	andvui, Mixteca
	tza, Georgian	... taka, Mon. ...	—	taxah, Pocon.
Mountain	kur, kar(a), Ak.	khalon, Mon. ...	kkollo, Aym. ...	
Hill	... taghez, Circ.	... tu, Mon.	... pata, Q.	.. tepe, Mex.
	mtha, Georg.	... takun, Kami ...	—	
		patouk, Shan....	—	
Stone	... taq(a), Ak.	... tamo, Camb.	... kak, Aym., Q....	te, Mex.
Rock	... kwa, Georg.	... kamou, Mon. ...	—	tete, Cora
Tree	... gu, iz, Ak.	... kai, Ann.	... khoka, Aym. ...	
	khe, Georg.	... kanoung, Mon. .	quenua, Aym....	
	—	akun, Kami ...		kan, Maya
Leaf	... potholi, Georg..	slak, Camb. ...	llakka, Aym. ...	
		thela,lah, Karen	lappi, Aym. ...	
	—	la, Ann. ...	—	
Field	... sa, Akkad	... sre, Camb. ...	—	
Garden	... gan(a), Akkad...	—	cancha, Q.	... zaca, Mex.
	kana, Georg. ...	—		
House,etc	uru, Akkad	...reuan, Siam		
	ziku, ,, ...	—	—	ngu, Othom.
	duk(u), Akkad..	phoun, Camb....	uta, ata, Aym., Q.	ata, Huas.
	sakhli, Georg....	ban, Siam	... puncu, Aym., Q.	otoch, Maya
Name	... mu, dara, Ak....	yamu, Mon.	... suti, Aym., Q...	sana, Mixte

F

	Western.	Indo-Chinese.	Peruvian.	Mexican, etc.
Name	... tsah, Circas. ...	maing, Karen...	—	
	—	amin, Burm. ...	—	
	—	chu, Siam ...	—	
Sheep	... lu, Akkad ...	—	llama, Q. ...	
	tzkwari, Georg..	—	ccaura, Aym. ...	
	heene, Circ., (la mb)	—	una, Aym.(lamb)	
Goat	... gizdin, Akkad ..	mea, Camb. ...	paca, Aym, ...	
	thkhavi, Georg..	khapa, Mon. ...	—	
Bull	... khar, la, Ak. ...	karau, Mon. ...	—	
Cow	... hari, Georg. ...	khaboi, Kami ...	—	
	dapara, Ak. ...	paren, Mon.,buf-	—	
	puri, Georgian..	— [falo	—	
Dog	... liku, Akkad ...	kala, Mon. ...	anokara, Aym..	cocochi, Tara.
	dzaghli, Geor....	khwe, Burm. ...	calatu, Q. ...	
	khah, Circas. ...	—	—	
Lion	... likmakh, Ak. ...	kala, Mon. ...	—	ocelo, Mex.
	lomi, Georg. ...	kya, Burm. ...	puma, Ak., Q....	
Wild sheep	... dara, Akkad ...	akkhoei, Camb..	taruca, Aym., Q.	
Bird	... khu, Akkad ...	—	quauh, Mex.	
	khathami, Geo..	khaton, Mon. ...	—	
	kattey, Circ. ...	kava ...	—	
Snake	... ti, sir, Ak. ...	tharun, Mon. ...	katari, Aym. ...	
Fish	... kha, khan, Ak. .	ka, Ann. ...	kañu, Aym. ...	cay, Poc.
	bat(a), Akkad...	para, Siam ...	—	
Good	... khiga, Akkad ...	chia, Camb. ...	asque, Aym. ...	
	kargi, Georg. ...	kha, Mon.	—	qualli, Mex.
	—	—	—	gala, Tara.
	—	gha, Karen, ...	—	khuta, Tara.
Bitter	... hur(i), Akkad ...	khah, Karen, B.	haru, Aym. ...	
Sour	... mekave, Geor. .	khom, Siam ...	—	
Black	... kug(i), Akkad...	khuaun, Camb..	—.	akahha, Maya
	mi, Akkad ...	mai, Burm. ...	chamaka, Aym..	
Red	... gusci, Akkad ...	gau, Karen ...	pako, Aym., Q..	cuz, Mex.
	—	hpakit, Mon. ...	—	kokoz, Mex.
Great	... enim, nun, Ak..	thanot. Mon. ...	hatun, Q. ...	noh, Maya
	makh, Akkad ...	miat, Burm. ...	—	nim, Poc.
	anta, Akkad ...	tau, Karen ...	—	na, ndi, Oth.
	atto, Circas. ...	—	—	
Give	... she, Akkad ...	sho, Ann. ...	chu, Aym. ...	caa, Maya
	ga? Akkad ...	ka, Mon. ...	ku, Q. ...	kia, Tara.
	mu, Akkad ...	pekya, Burm. ...	—	maka, Mex.
Run	... riati, Ak. ...	garitaa[aara], Mon.	huayra, Q. ...	
Flow	... rli, Georg. ...	pre, Burm. ...	[puri, Q.] ...	
Go	... —	aara, Mon. ...	[humi, Aym.,Q.]	huma, Tara.
Speak	... kaka, Ak. ...	nikay, Camb. ...	—	ynqui, Poc.
	laparako, Geor..	hankai, Mon. ...	arusi, Aym. ...	
	—	chho, Burm. ...	rima, Q. ...	
	—	hanmarai, Mon..	—	
Eat	... ka, Ak. ...	chhan, Camb....	mancana, Aym..	[Tava.
	ja, Georg. ...	cha, Burm. ...	—	qua, Cora, Mex.,
	—	au, Ann. ...	—	hanal, Maya
Drink	... ka, Ak. ...	kenn, Siam ...	—	hindi, Mixteca
	nak, Ak. ...	thou, Mon. ...	—	chia, Mex.
	sua, Georg. ...	sok, Burm. ...	—	
Die	... khan, khut, Ak.	mathi, Karen ...	amaya, Aym. ...	muechit, Ceva
Kill	... be, ba, bat, Ak..	kha, Siam ...	—	miquiz, Mex.
.	sikua, Georg. ...	—	—	mukiki, Tara.
Cut	... kud, khas, Ak...	—	cuta, Aym. ...	

	Western.	Indo-Chinese.	Peruvian.	Mexican, etc.
Break	... rc, Georg.	... rei, Camb.	... rutu, Q.	...
Cry	... tuq(a), Ak.	... toui, Camb.	... huaca	...
Weep	... —	khok, Ann.	...	—
Place	... ka, khash, Ak....	—	chura, Q.	...
Put	... ko, thsqo, Geor.	—	cancha, Q.	...
Rise	... ri, Ak.	... mhrang, Burm .	hatari, Q.	...
Raise	... aka, Ak.	... heka, Karen	... hucaro, Q.	...
Many	... mes, Ak.	... husamia, Burm.	—	miec, Mex.
All	... ka, Ak.	... ahmah, Karen	.. [naka, Aym.]	...
	koweli, Geor. ...	—	[kuna, Q]	...
No, not...	nu, Ak.	... pnoom, Camb....	hani, Aym.	...
Negative.	nu, Geor.	... ma, Burm., etc..	ma, Aym., Q.	... mao, Maya
	—	na, Kumi ...	—	ma, Poc.

The pronouns are of such varied type and distribution that
only a few selections are offered.

	Western.	Indo-Chinese.	Peruvian.	Mexican, etc.
I, me	... mu, idbi, Ak....	awai, Mon. ...	—	ma, Oth.
	mi, Georg. ...	—	—	
	—	nyo, Angka	... na, Aym.	... nuga, Oth.
	—	nga, Burm.	... noca, Q.	... ne, Mex.
	—	kha, Siam., etc..	—	
Thou	... zu, Ak.	... tua, Siam.	... -ta, Aym.	... tata, Huas.
	shen, Geor.	... tha, Karen ...	—	mi, Totonaca
	mun, men, Ak..	—.	—	timo, Mex.
	weyroo, Circ. ...	bai, Mon. ...	—	pe, Cora
	—	ba, Angka ...	—	pu, Tara.
	—	nah, Karen	... nqui, Q.	... nugui, Oth.
He	... ni, bi, Ak.	... no, Ann.	... hupa, Aym.	... nunu, Oth.
	[ni,bi,plur.Geo.]	wa.	... pay, Q.	... bi, Oth.
	igi, misi, Geor..	ni, Khyeng	... ni, Aym,	...
	—	pho, Angka	... n, Q.	...
We	... me, Ak. ...	—	—	ma, Oth.
	—	—	—	tame, Tara
Plurals	... -nene, Ak.	... -aen, Siam	... kuna, Q.	... nana, Huas.
	-no, Ak.	... -niht, Shan.	... naka, Aym.	...
	-ni, Georg. ...	—	—	
	-bi, Georg.	... tau, Mon.	... pay, Aym.	... te, Cora
	-th, Georg.	... dah, Karen	...	
1...	... id, Ak.	... moe, Camb.	... mai, Aym.	... ce, Mex.
	zee, Circas.	... mway, Mon.	... huc, suc, Q.	... tam, Totomaca
	erthi, Geor.	... mot., Ann.	...	
	—	tach, Burm.	...	
	—	ter, Karen	...	
2...	... bi, Ak.	... bar, Camb.	... pa, Aym.	... poa, Cora
	kas, Ak.	... pa, Mon.	... yscay, Q.	... ome, Mex.
	oh, Circas.	... ki, Karen	...	yoho, Oth.
	ori, Georg.	... kai, Angka	...	os, Tara.
3...	... essa, Ak.	... sung, thou, Bur.	kimsa, Aym., Q.	osh, Huas.
	sami, Georg.	... sam, Siam	...	osh, Maya
	shee, Circas.	... htsan. Shan.	...	
	—	pah, Camb.	...	ba, Tara.
	—	pe, Mon.	...	—
4 ..	... sana, Ak.	... si, Siam	... pusi, Aym.	...
	—	htse, Shan.	...	—
	—	tse, Angka	...	—
	—	pon, Mon.	...	—
	—	buan, Camb. ...	—	

Western.	Indo-Chinese.	Peruvian.	Mexican, etc.
5... ...sha, Ak.	... ha, Siam, Shan.	ppiska, Aym., Q.	
para, Ak.	... patson, Mon. ...	—	
tpey, Circ.	... panggna, Kami.	—	
6... ...as, Ak.	... sau, Ann.	... socta, Aym., Q..	
shoo, Circas.	... sauk, Khyeng. .	—	
ekusi, Georg. ...	—	—	

DISCUSSION.

Consul T. J. HUTCHINSON being called on by the President, said he was afraid to enter into this discussion in commenting on the deep philological research displayed by Dr. Hyde Clarke, or on the extensive knowledge of warlike instruments, for which Colonel Lane is so well known. But he had his doubts about the possibility of learning the grammatical formations of languages from such tribes as those Dr. Clarke spoke of in Western Africa. Their dialects were all unwritten, and it had been observed by Captain Adams, that the tower of Babel might have been built on the West coast of Africa, so numerous and varied were the idioms spoken there. For his own part he believed in what we have to learn of the anthropology of past people, much more from their works of art, than from what should be considered as guesses at philology. He was happy to tell the meeting that the collection of copper implements, of cloth, of pottery-ware resembling that excavated from Priam's Ilium, by Dr. Henry Schliemann, of silver works of art, and other matters, brought by him from Peru, were now arranged at the Bethnal Green Museum, and in a short time the catalogue of them would be ready.

Dr. LEITNER gave an account of the origin, progress, system, and present attitude of the Indo-Germanic School of Philology, and considered that Dr. Hyde Clarke's researches, which he illustrated by coincidences derived from Arabic and his own Dardu discoveries, as well as those of all scholars and independent inquirers, deserved every encouragement for the sake of the cause of truth, and as a protest against the literary terrorism exercised by a set of Sanscritists, who now monopolised attention in certain leading societies and journals, erroneously supposed to be devoted to impartial investigations. The collection of material, historical, ethnological and other, was far more important than the preservation of this or that philological theory. We were on the mere threshold of the science of language; the Indo-Germanic group was, with some stretching, scientifically classified, whilst the affinities of the Shemitic languages had never been doubted. The terms, however, of "Turanian" and even of "Hamitic" were a mere euphuism to express the absolute ignorance of our present philologers regarding the position to be assigned to that vast number of languages which yet remained insufficiently examined or unknown.

Mr. R. G. HALIBURTON said : I have listened to this discussion with much pleasure, not only on account of the importance of the subject before us, but also on account of the liberal spirit which has been evinced, for bigotry unfortunately is not confined to theologians, but is often as unreasoning and intolerant in science as it is in religion. Mr. Clarke's conclusion that there has been a connection between the religions and civilizations of the new and old worlds has been confirmed by a very careful investigation of my own, extending over twenty years, into the identities existing between the calendars, festivals, and astronomical ideas of savage races in America, Polynesia, Africa, and Asia. These coincidences are very striking and very conclusive, and I hope before long to submit the result of my labours to the notice of the public. There are proofs that there must have been repeated intercommunication between the races of the new and the old worlds prior to the days of Columbus. So evident is this conclusion that some writers have tried to establish that the origin of the religions and the civilisation of the old world must be sought in America. We have in the new world monuments of the stone age similar to those found in Denmark and elsewhere. We have coincidences in the calendars of the races inhabiting both continents which cannot be accidental. In architecture the resemblances are most striking. The grouping of Mexican pyramids I have found to be the same as that observable in Egypt, and a similar symbolism is to be traced in some of the groups of mounds in the new world, which is to be noticed in prehistoric structures of the old. We have Cyclopean masonry in Peru, and symbols which are conspicuous in the temples of the old world. There can be no doubt that we are on the eve of important discoveries, and Mr. Hyde Clarke by his valuable paper has pointed out very clearly how much we have to learn, and how much remains to reward the labours of the Anthropological Institute.

Mr. J. JEREMIAH, Jun., said, in reference to the remarks of Mr. Haliburton, in relation to his labours in American archæology, and his conclusions respecting the astronomical characteristics of the Mexican and Egyptian pyramids, that in a work in his collection, entitled "The Lost Solar System of the Ancients Discovered," by a Mr. John Wilson, published (in two volumes) as far back as 1856, the same conclusions are stated; but how far correct he was not this evening prepared to say. The work abounds with apparently accurate measurements of all the then known great megalithic monuments in Europe, Asia, Africa, and America, and elaborately detailed and worked out, to show that they were constructed in accordance with the Oriental astronomical system, and it may be remarked that the valuable paper we have listened to goes very far to support some of Wilson's arguments. It seems a pity that the labours of years at times turns out to be already forestalled in the main by some unknown work published years ago, as in the case of the honourable gentleman who preceded me. Mr. Hyde Clarke has proceeded upon strictly scientific grounds, and whether we premise the descent of the human family from one or more pairs, his researches will always afford the student much material for carrying on the impartial study of the history of man in the vast continent of America, and assist the comparative study of the progress of the human mind in every part of the ancient world.

Colonel LANE FOX, Senor de la ROSA, and the PRESIDENT also made some remarks.

======

Mr. R. G. Halliburton's Discovery of the Year of the Pleiades.

Mr. Halliburton states, that in the Mexican pyramids, he has found the grouping to be the same as that observable in Egypt (the three groups), and in some of the groups of mounds of the new world.

This does not state the whole truth of a most important discovery, which will lead to a knowledge of the obscure origin of the Egyptian system of learning, and that of the American monuments. It is something far older than the Egyptian system, hoar as that is in antiquity, and will place the earlier American moundbuilding migrations, at a very early period far beyond that of the Sumerians, chiefly referred to by me.

In the pyramids mentioned, there is one large (Sun) pyramid, one smaller (Moon) pyramid, and 7 little pyramids, grouped, as I observed, 3 in a trinity with the Sun pyramid and 4 with the Moon pyramid. Mr. Halliburton has not yet been able to explain this to me, but the symbolism must have its value.

The connection of the 7 has, however, been established by Mr. Halliburton that they are the seven Pleiades of the Bull. When these 7 in the middle of November are in a line with the 5 of the Bull, and these with the 3 in Orion and with the Dog Star, we have a series of 1, 3, 5, and 7, and the epoch of a prehistoric new year, marked by the festival of the dead. The Pleiades, constituting a cross or Tau, are also recognised as a paradise of the souls of men.

On the day of the Pleiades, festivals are still held throughout the world. This great day was also one of human sacrifice.

Traces of its observance are almost universal in the Old World and the New, and in the passage of communication in the Feejee Islands.

A whole volume of symbolism is to be deduced not only from the myths, but from the numbers of 3, 5, and 7, and the unrolling of which will give us new and trustworthy results.

These investigations will probably assist us in arriving at the animal origin of the constellations and signs of the zodiac. This may be based on the facts at pp. 24 and 25.

Note on P. 38.

Early Metal Working.

Very valuable materials on early metal working and its synchronism with comparative mythology, will be found in the papers of Miss A. Buckland, in the Journal of the Anthropological Institute and the Westminster Review for January.

MEMOIR ON THE COMPARATIVE GRAMMAR OF EGYPTIAN, COPTIC, AND UDE,

By HYDE CLARKE.

LONDON :

TRÜBNER & CO., 57 & 59, LUDGATE HILL.

1873.

Price 3s. 6d.

www.ingramcontent.com/pod-product-compliance
Lightning Source LLC
Chambersburg PA
CBHW031450270326
41930CB00007B/939